# ABRAHAM
## FOLLOWING GOD'S PROMISE

## Also available in the Studies in Faithful Living Series

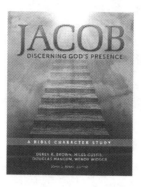

*Jacob: Discerning God's Presence*

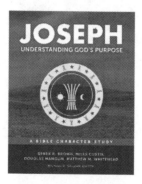

*Joseph: Understanding God's Purpose*

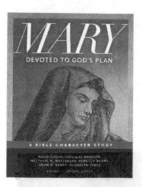

*Mary: Devoted to God's Plan*

**For updates on this series, visit LexhamPress.com/SFL**

# ABRAHAM
## FOLLOWING GOD'S PROMISE

Studies in Faithful Living

Miles Custis
Douglas Mangum
Matthew M. Whitehead

**Editor and Coauthor**

Michael R. Grigoni

LEXHAM PRESS

*Abraham: Following God's Promise*
Studies in Faithful Living

ISBN 978-1-57799581-4

Assistant Editors: Rebecca Brant, Jessi Strong, Elizabeth Vince, Britt Rogers
Cover Design: Jim LePage, Lyndsey Plute, Christine Gerhart, Brittany VanErem
Typesetting: ProjectLuz.com

# TABLE OF CONTENTS

# INTRODUCTION

In the life of faith, we often hear that the hardest step to take is the very first one. Abraham's story opens with such a step, as God tells him, without invitation or warning, to "go ... to the land that I will show you" (Gen 12:1). While Abraham responds in faith to this call, beginning one of the great narratives of the Bible, his subsequent steps do not get easier. His story teaches us something profound: that the life of faith is a journey made up of a series of "first steps." While each of these steps brings us closer to the fulfillment of God's promises, they don't necessarily lead us farther away from the challenges and struggles involved with moving ahead.

Looking at the "steps" that make up the lives of characters like Abraham is one way to read and engage with the story of the Bible. This is the approach taken by the Studies in Faithful Living series. This series looks closely at the lives of those who lived in faithful response to God's call. Each volume examines the events of these characters' lives in order to draw out the lessons their faithful responses provide for us. In studying God's Word in this way, we can learn to model those who have gone before us and grow in our efforts to model Christ. In doing so, we participate in the story the Bible narrates for us: God's redeeming work in those he created in his image—a story of redemption that continues in the lives of those who respond to him today.

Although the Bible often depicts Abraham as an exalted figure, his journey of faith resembles our own. Along with the glory of his victories, the Bible fully describes the scandalous details of his failures. It does not hide Abraham's shortcomings; instead, it recounts these examples of failure so that we might have hope. In Abraham, we observe someone uniquely chosen to receive a grand promise: that he would become the father of a great nation and a channel of blessing to the world. Abraham embraced this promise, but it was 25 years before he saw it realized. As he waited on God, he battled fear, anxiety, and doubt. In Abraham, we see a reflection of ourselves.

Chapter 1 begins with an examination of Abraham's response to God's call. In Chapter 2, we witness the beginning of Abraham's battle with fear as he leads Sarah into deception. Chapter 3 relates one of Abraham's greatest successes following God's reassurance of his promises: military victory and royal blessing. In Chapter 4, we find Abraham struggling deeply with doubt as he and Sarah turn to Hagar to provide an heir. We also consider the covenant ritual through which God reconfirms his promise. In Chapter 5, God further reveals his promise by giving Abraham the sign of circumcision. Abraham boldly bargains with God over the inhabitants of Sodom in Chapter 6. In Chapter 7, Abraham relapses into old sin. Chapter 8 considers God's command that Abraham sacrifice his son, Isaac. In this chapter, we also find Abraham's finest hour and the reason that he's often remembered as the model of faithful living.

To help you dig deeper into the biblical stories, we've arranged each chapter into five sections. In *Setting the Stage*, we introduce the theme of the chapter and the significant literary, historical, and cultural details of the story at hand. Then, *A Closer Look* illuminates the narrative by walking you through the story itself. *Throughout the Bible* connects the Old and New Testaments and shows how people have remembered, retold, and relied upon these stories at various points in biblical history. *Beyond the Bible* accomplishes a similar task by locating the biblical stories within various historical contexts. This leads into the *Application*, where we discuss the relevance of Abraham's experiences for our lives today. Application and reflection questions conclude each chapter to help you reflect upon and internalize what you've read.

Abraham's story isn't that different from ours. It's about responding to God's call, journeying with him through life, facing challenges, and growing as a result of them. Fundamentally, it's about the change that occurs because of redemption. In Abraham's life, this change is signified by God changing his name from "Abram" to "Abraham" (Gen 17, discussed in Chapter 5). Because of its significance, we've retained this distinction in this book: Chapters 1–4 use "Abram," and chapters 5–8 use "Abraham." His new identity serves as a daily reminder of God's promises, just like our new identity in Christ does for us.

Portraits of faithful living look different depending upon the character. The same principle is true in our walks with God today. He uses our unique personalities and experiences to forge us into the people he wants us to be. But his role in the process is always the same: He who began a good work in us will complete it (Phil 1:6). As we persistently pursue God in our daily lives, we can be confident that he is perfectly and persistently accomplishing his plan for the redemption of the world.

## CHAPTER 1

# STEPPING OUT IN FAITH

*Read Genesis 11:27–12:9.*

## SETTING THE STAGE

**Theme.** What would *you* do if God came for you—if out of the blue, he said, "I need you to pick up and move. Get your stuff together. I'll tell you where to go later." Imagine explaining this to your spouse, parents, or best friend. They would look at you like you were crazy. They would protest. They would doubt you had really talked to God. They'd do their best to talk you out of it. Yet God called Abram in exactly this way.

In fact, Abram's situation was even more complicated. He wasn't an eager young man looking for adventure. The Bible tells us he was 75 years old when God singled him out and told him to move, promising him a legacy in exchange for his obedience. While Sarai, his wife, may have protested, the story simply shows Abram quietly obeying God's call, leaving for an unknown land where he would supposedly experience the promised blessing.

As the story unfolds, we find that God's promised blessing sits at the heart of Abram's story (whom God later renames Abraham). Abram responded to God's call because of his hope in this future blessing. His expectation that God would fulfill his word underscored everything he did. In fact, Abram may have responded in faith because God promised him the one thing he still lacked: a son. In this way, Abram's story becomes more than the account of the patriarch; it illustrates the OT expectation of the One who would one day restore God's relationship with his people (Gal 4:4–5).

Like Abram, we also respond in faith to God's call—the one heard through the voice of his Son.

**Literary Context.** The introduction of Abram represents a major turning point in the story of Genesis. God's previous interactions with humanity, from Adam to the Babel event, were marked by discord and conflict. Abram's responsive acceptance of God contrasted sharply with humanity's continual resistance (except for Noah; see Gen 6:9–8:22). With Abram, God finally found someone who embraced his offer of blessing in exchange for obedience.

With Abram, God also narrowed his focus. Rather than deal with humanity in general, he began to work through a specifically *chosen* people. And yet, God's promise to Abram would affect all of humanity. While he blessed Abram as an individual, the whole world would receive divine blessing through Abram (Gen 12:2–3). This pivotal point in the biblical narrative influences everything that follows in the story of Abram's life.

> **Quick Bit:** The Bible is filled with genealogies. Some explain where the nations of the known world or an immediate region came from (e.g., Gen 10). Others help move the biblical story from one major character to the next (e.g., Gen 5). The genealogy that leads up to Abram moves the story from the time of Noah up to Abram, the next major figure of Genesis (see Gen 10; 11:10–26).

We first encounter Abram in Genesis 11, which introduces his family and provides the backstory to the events of Genesis 12 (see Gen 11:27–32). Abram was part of a seminomadic clan led by his father, Terah. The clan included Abram's brothers, Nahor and Haran; Abram's nephew, Lot; Nahor's wife, Milcah; and Abram's wife, Sarai. This brief narrative introduces people and locations that will be important later in Genesis—especially when Abram's descendants interacted with his extended family in northern Mesopotamia.

**Historical & Cultural Background.** Genesis 11:27–32 introduces three key locations: Ur of the Chaldeans, Haran, and Canaan. Abram's birthplace, "Ur of the Chaldeans," refers either to a large ancient city in southern Mesopotamia or a smaller trading center in northwest Mesopotamia. Clues from elsewhere in Abram's story suggest he viewed the region around Haran in northwest Mesopotamia as his homeland (Gen 24:4–7), but later biblical texts connect him to southern Mesopotamia because of the mention of "Chaldeans" in Genesis 11:28. Most biblical references to Chaldeans use the name as a synonym for the Babylonians, the inhabitants of Babylon—a major city in south central Mesopotamia (Isa 13:19; 47:1). Given this, Abram's migration from southern Mesopotamia to Canaan was later believed to foreshadow the experience of Jews returning from Babylonian exile.

Haran was a city on the upper Euphrates River in northwestern Mesopotamia. On the way from Ur to Canaan, Terah and the rest of the clan settled in Haran. The story provides no explanation as to why they interrupted their journey to Canaan in this way. Terah lived his final days in Haran (Gen 11:31–32).

Canaan was the promised land, the region that would one day become Israelite territory. In introducing Canaan here, Genesis 11:27–32 indicates that Abram's story is the story of Israel's beginning. Three locations within Canaan are specifically mentioned throughout Abram's story: Shechem, Bethel, and the Negev. Together, these locations represent the primary areas that Abram and his descendants later occupied in Genesis. They also represent the major strongholds of future Israelite control.

Shechem was located in the central hill country of Israel and appears to have served as a capital city at times in Israel's history (Josh 24; 1 Kgs 12). Bethel was an ancient Canaanite sacred site in the hill country of Israel (south of Shechem but north of Jerusalem). After the kingdoms of Israel and Judah split (1 Kgs 12), Bethel sat just north of Judah at Israel's southern border. The third territory—the Negev—was the southernmost region of Canaan; it later became the southern border region of Judah. In highlighting these three locations, Genesis highlights Abram's ancient presence in the heart of what would become Israelite territory, and it illustrates the significance of God's promise of land and a son to a wandering, barren couple.

## A CLOSER LOOK

Reading quickly over the short account of Genesis 12:1–9 may cause us to miss the implications of the events. On the surface, the story is clear:

God called, and Abram answered with obedience. But imagine Abram in the midst of this situation, trying to explain to his family what God told him to do. How did Sarai respond? Did she question whether he really heard from God? Who was this God anyway? And why did he choose Abram?

> **Quick Bit:** The Hebrew word *moledeth* can be used to refer to someone's homeland (Ruth 2:11; Jer 22:10), birthplace (Jer 46:16; Ezek 16:3), relatives (Gen 43:7; Num 10:30), or children (Gen 48:6). Aside from its use in Genesis 12:1, the word occurs eight more times in Genesis. Unfortunately, "birthplace" and "relatives" work equally well in many of the contexts where *moledeth* occurs. However, in Genesis 12:1 "birthplace" makes more sense than "relatives" since "father's house" at the end of the list clearly indicates Abram's extended family. Abram was called to leave behind his current home, his birthplace, and his family to go where God might lead.

At this point in the story, the Bible hasn't told us anything about Abram or about what kind of man he was. With Noah, the last person God singled out, the Bible at least indicates that he was "a righteous man" (Gen 6:9). We are not told exactly when Abram received the call. It may have occurred before he left Ur or after his father died in Haran—the passage is silent on this point.[1] But what's ultimately important is that God commanded Abram to leave his "land," his *moledeth*, and his "father's house" (Gen 12:1 ESV). Whether the Hebrew word *moledeth* refers to Abram's relatives or to his birthplace (it could refer to either), God clearly called Abram from the familiar to the unknown.

The lack of detail in God's instruction for Abram to go "to the land that I will show you" indicates Abram's faith: He packed up and left in response to the call, blindly trusting God to lead him. Abram did not verbally respond to God's address. He never asked where he should go or how he would know when he got there.

However, God's words would have struck Abram as odd—leave your homeland and family, you will become a great nation—especially his final statement, "all families of the earth will be blessed in you" (Gen 12:3). How could all families on earth be blessed through one man? Abram didn't know the details of how these events would unfold, but he believed the promise and obeyed. God promised to lead him to a new land and provide him with children, to bless his journey and provide for his well-being. Abram believed, prepared his family and possessions, and got on the road to Canaan.

> **Quick Bit:** The Hebrew word *nephesh* is an extremely common yet complicated term. In the Bible, the word has a wide range of reference, from actual living beings to concepts like human desires or appetites. The Bible regularly uses the word in reference to the soul or the intangible life force when contrasting "flesh" (physical) with "soul" (spiritual) (Deut 12:23; Isa 10:18). But in the book of Genesis, the term often has the simple meaning of "any living being" (Gen 1:20; 2:7, 19).

Abram must have been leading a sizable caravan. The story tells us that he took his wife, Sarai, his nephew, Lot, all their possessions, "and all the persons they had acquired in Haran" (Gen 12:5). The Hebrew word for "persons" is *nephesh*, a word often translated as "souls." Some interpretations of Abram's life take the appearance of this word as proof that Abram's business in Haran was converting souls to follow the one true God (see "Beyond the Bible").

Once in Canaan, Abram traveled to Shechem, one of three main areas where he stopped to build an altar to worship God (compare Gen 35:4; Josh 24:26). God expanded on his promise to Abram at the oak near Shechem. While in his first announcement, God told Abram to go, promising to bless him (Gen 12:1–3), in this second announcement, he confirmed that Abram was in the right place by promising to give this very land to his descendants (Gen 12:7). Once again, Abram responded with actions, not speech. He built an altar, worshiped God, and continued to explore the land, building another altar near Bethel and moving still farther south "toward the Negev" (Gen 12:9).

While the absence of any spoken response to God is remarkable, Abram's actions provided greater evidence of his strong faith than words ever could. His acts of obedience not only marked a new beginning for Abram, they marked a new beginning for God's relationship with humanity. Through Abram's faithful response, God's care and concern for the entire world became intimately linked to his care and concern for Abram and his descendants. And yet, at this point in the story, much of this remains to be seen. Sarai was barren, and Abram, advanced in age, still had many lessons to learn about God's plan, provision, and purpose.

# THROUGHOUT THE BIBLE

Abram's faithful response to God influenced the efforts of later biblical writers as they, too, struggled to balance faithful obedience to God with fear of the unknown. Generations after Abram, his descendants, the Israelites, faced the daunting prospect of a journey from Mesopotamia back to the promised land: the return from Babylonian exile. The prophets encouraged the Israelites by reminding them of God's faithfulness to Abram, especially since their journey resembled his course from Ur to Canaan (Mic 7:19–20; Isa 51:2–3). For many Israelites, life continued to be hard at the journey's end. As at the beginning of their journey, they reflected on how God faithfully provided for Abram throughout his experience and journey (Neh 9:7).

> **Quick Bit:** In 586 BC, the Babylonians destroyed Jerusalem and the temple, carrying off most of the Jewish population to Babylon as exiles (2 Kgs 25:8–11). This event is called the "Babylonian exile" or, more commonly, "the exile." It marks a turning point in Israel's relationship with God since the survivors of the exile realized that Israel's long pattern of disobedience to him led to their punishment (Neh 9:1–38). After decades in Babylon, Jewish settlers began returning to Palestine after the Persian king Cyrus gave them permission to resettle their homeland in 539 BC (Ezra 1:1–4).

When NT writers reflected on the faith of their ancestors, Abram's obedience to God's call was a constant source of reassurance (Acts 7:2–4; Heb 11:8). Stephen began his account of Israel's history of disobedience to God by highlighting Abram's obedience (Acts 7:2–8). The writer of Hebrews emphasized that Abram went "not knowing where he was going" (Heb 11:8). Just as Abram's journey served to reassure the Israelites returning from exile, his actions provided a model of exemplary faith for the early church.

Jesus himself brought together Abram's story and the story of the world's salvation in saying "Abraham your father rejoiced that he would see my day, and he saw it and was glad" (John 8:56). Here, Jesus exhorted his Jewish audience to model Abram by looking *ahead* to the fulfillment of God's plan of salvation—a plan that Christ himself fulfilled before their very eyes. Instead, the Jews opposing Jesus looked to the past, living by their tradition and idolizing Abram.

Traditions in the NT (and beyond) show how some Jews from ancient times substituted Abram's model of living faith with a system of rules. This led them to impose their understanding of righteousness and merit onto Abram's life. It also led them to trust in their genealogical relationship to Abram more than their relationship to God (Matt 3:9; John 8:39-40). Jesus' words help remind us that the "heroes of faith" should always lead us toward the ultimate fulfillment of God's words, which is Christ.

## BEYOND THE BIBLE

For ancient Bible readers, Abram's backstory from Genesis 11:27–12:3 wasn't enough. Yes, God called him to be a "great nation"—but why? Was there something special about Abram that led God to choose him instead of someone else? We may wonder the same thing when we think about someone in church ministry or leadership. Why did he or she receive a call rather than someone else? What's so special about that person?

Ancient Jewish interpreters had similar questions about Abram's story. To make sense of his calling, they imagined that Abram must have had a certain degree of merit—at least enough to attract God's attention. As a result, they embellished Abram's backstory. The idea that God called Abram simply because he wanted to, apart from Abram's merit, was unfathomable. It required them to accept Abram's flawed humanity, an image that conflicted with their tradition of viewing Abram as the ultimate model of faith.

The ancient Jewish commentary *Genesis Rabbah* provides many examples of how Jewish interpreters venerated Abram. Written over the first 500 years after Christ, *Genesis Rabbah* contains extensive interpretations of the book of Genesis. It explains Abram's role in restoring righteousness to the world after Adam's fall brought sin into the world:

> Perhaps in the proper order of things, Abraham should have been the first man created, not Adam. God, however, foresaw the fall of the first man, and if Abraham had been the first man and had fallen, there would have been no one after him to restore righteousness to the world; whereas after Adam's fall came Abraham, who established in the world the knowledge of God. As a builder puts the strongest beam in the centre of the building, so as to support the structure at both ends, so Abraham was the strong beam carrying the burden of the generations that existed before him and that came after him. (Genesis Rabbah 14)[2]

The authors of *Genesis Rabbah* clearly recognized the importance of Abram's response to God's call. They viewed Abram's role as an integral part of God's plan for the salvation of humanity. But their focus was on Abram's righteousness, not God's faithfulness to Abram. For these interpreters, Abram's legacy overshadowed the action of God himself.

The *Babylonian Talmud*, a Jewish collection of legal and biblical interpretations, also reflects the great weight that rabbinic interpreters placed on Abram's merit:

> The day on which our father, Abraham, died, all of the principal authorities of the nations of the world formed a line and said, "Woe is the world that has lost its leader, woe to the ship that has lost its helmsman." (b. B. Bat. 91A–B)[3]

Other ancient Jewish texts further elaborated on Abram's merit by imaginatively describing the days of his youth. They depict him as an insightful young man who, despite living in an age of idol worship, realized the truth that there is just one God.[4] These stories present Abram as having worshiped the true God and battled against idol worship in his homeland—all before God called him. In these accounts, Abram's father sold idols, but Abram crippled the family business by mocking potential customers for worshiping idols of stone—objects that had been made that very day:

... if any one accosted Abraham, to buy an idol from him, and asked him the price, he would answer, "Three manehs," and then question in turn, "How old art thou?" "Thirty years," the reply would be. "Thou art thirty years of age, and yet thou wouldst worship this idol which I made but to-day?" The man would depart and go his way ... [5]

Since nothing in the biblical account explains why God selected Abram to father a "great nation," the writers of these stories had to come up with an explanation that made sense of the question, "What type of person is good enough for God?" In the same way, we often focus on what we can do or who we can emulate to make ourselves more acceptable to God. Instead, our focus should be on Jesus, the promised Son of God who fulfilled the worldwide blessing initiated with Abram's call (Matt 1:1–17). Like the ancient writers who focused on Abram, we sometimes miss what God is doing today or will do tomorrow by focusing on his past action. We can emulate Abram by stepping out in faith, recognizing that God chooses us and continues to work with us because of his merit, not ours.

# APPLICATION

Sometimes the hardest step of faith is the very first one. Every day leads us to a crossroads at which we must choose between faith in God's promises and fear of the unknown. In Genesis 12:1–9, Abram leaned fully on his faith, trusting in God and his promise that he would be blessed and play a role in the blessing of the whole world. While Abram did not know, at this point, how God would bring about this plan, his later attempts to ensure the success of God's promise suggest he may have understood that worldwide blessing was in some way dependent on his survival. As one writer put it, "Abraham was the strong beam carrying the burden of the generations that existed before him and that came after him."[6]

In retrospect, we can see that Abram had nothing to fear; God ensured the fulfillment of his promise. But Abram's fears and doubts help us reflect on our own relationship to God's call and promise in our lives. When we get caught up in what we think we need to do for God in order to be worthy of him, we may lose sight of the only things we truly need to do: trust in his promise, accept his call, and surrender our doubts, fears, and insecurities.

Just like our own walks, Abram's journey of faith was not perfect. Yet even though Abram continued to be nagged by doubt and fear, he kept looking ahead to where God was leading him. The Apostle Paul used Abram's life to draw out the same truth: A true child of Abram lives by faith in the promised Son, who brings blessing to the entire world (Gal 3:6–9). The message of Abram's life points to this essential truth of the gospel: We must live by faith in God, no matter what.

# DISCUSSION

## A Closer Look

1. Have you ever felt torn, like Abram, between what you felt God was calling you to do and what your friends, family, or neighbors expected you to do? How did you respond? What types of pressures did you face from those who questioned your call?

_____

_____

2. Consider the time and energy Abram would have had to invest in building an altar and offering sacrifice for worship. How did he honor God with outward acts that reflected his inward faith? While worship today doesn't always require physical effort on our part, it could. In what ways could you outwardly and physically respond to God in worship?

_____

_____

## Throughout the Bible

1. It's easy to feel disconnected from the people God worked through in biblical times. Does the Bible's emphasis on God's past faithfulness encourage or frustrate you? What Bible verses, hymns, or praise songs help renew your faith in times of struggle?

_____

_____

2. Reflect on an occasion when God led you to the right place at the right time. Was your experience like Abram's, with God leading in a clear and obvious way? If you couldn't see his hand in the events of that time, how did you react?

_____

_____

**Beyond the Bible**

1. We can learn a lot about faith from watching the faithful, but there's a risk. Have you ever found that you compare yourself to other believers and perhaps idolize those who seem to have an "ideal" faith? What can we do to maintain balance—appreciating those God has put in our lives to learn from while not losing sight of his hand in all things?

_____

_____

_____

2. Have you ever struggled to accept God's grace? Did you find it hard to believe that he loves and accepts you as you are? How have you learned to trust God's love for you?

_____

_____

**Application**

1. We all resist God's nudges and fight to stay within our own comfort zones. Have you ever caught yourself intentionally holding back when you felt called to step out in faith? Why might God keep trying to draw you toward something new and unknown?

_____

_____

_____

2. Think about a time when you felt you had stepped out in faith, but things quickly started to take a wrong turn. How did you react? Did you try to hang on to what you thought God had promised?

_____

_____

_____

## CHAPTER 2

# FEAR VERSUS FAITH

*Read Genesis 12:10-20.*

## SETTING THE STAGE

**Theme.** We often talk about trusting God's promises, but rarely does trusting God involve risking our lives. Yet this was the situation Abram faced in Genesis 12:10-20. Confronted with difficult circumstances, Abram had to decide whether to trust in God's promises or take matters into his own hands.

We've all experienced this: One minute we're confidently striding along God's path for our lives, and the next we find ourselves at a crossroads with no markers and no sense of direction. Abram came to such a crossroads not long after arriving in Canaan. Just as he and Sarai had settled in their new home, severe famine struck the land. Abram was forced to choose: remain in the land of promise and risk death by starvation, or relocate temporarily to Egypt and risk death at the hand of foreign enemies. Abram had just received God's promise that he would become a "great nation" (Gen 12:2), but that future now appeared to be in jeopardy. Rather than standing firm in faith, Abram allowed fear to sway him, and he chose Egypt over God's promise. Yet, as the Bible demonstrates again and again, God remains faithful to his promise and his people, despite their decisions.

**Historical & Cultural Background.** Famines were not unusual in ancient Mesopotamia. Often caused by drought, famines jeopardized the food supplies of animals and people alike, and they quickly became a matter of life and death. Agriculture in Egypt was less dependent on rain than agriculture in Canaan: The regular flooding of the Nile provided water for crops. During times of famine, people living in Canaan often traveled to Egypt, knowing they would likely find food there. Egyptian tomb carvings from around the 20th century BC such as the Beni Hasan mural show Semitic people traveling to Egypt.

The biblical accounts provide several examples of famines displacing God's people. For example, famine forced Abram's son, Isaac, to travel to Gerar (Gen 26:1), and a more severe famine forced Isaac's son, Jacob, and his family to move to Egypt when Joseph was in power (Gen 41–47; compare Ruth 1:1).

Ancient Near Eastern documents also speak of the severity of famines and thus help us understand the anxiety and worry Abram may have experienced. For example, an Egyptian document from the end of the 13th century BC describes Bedouin shepherds from Edom traveling to Per-Atum (probably the biblical Pithom) to keep their livestock alive: "We have finished letting the Bedouin tribes of Edom pass … to the pools of Per-Atum of Mer-ne-Ptah Hotep-hir-Maat … to keep them alive and to keep their cattle alive, through the great ka of Pharaoh—life, prosperity, health!"[1]

An Egyptian document called "The Admonitions of Ipuwer" (probably written before 2000 BC) describes the effects of famine:

> Lo, [one eats] herbs, washed down with water,
> Birds find neither fruit nor herbs,
> One takes [ ] from the mouth of pigs,
> No face is bright … hunger.
> Lo, grain is lacking on all sides,
> One is stripped of clothes,
> Unanointed with oil,
> Everyone says, "There's nothing."
> The storehouse is bare,
> Its keeper stretched on the ground.[2]

Such accounts help us understand Abram's decision to take matters into his own hands and travel to Egypt; they demonstrate that famine was an issue of life and death in the ancient world. Since the residents of Canaan often found refuge from famine in Egypt, staying in Canaan would have been illogical to Abram and Sarai.

**Literary Context.** Still, Abram's decision to travel to Egypt revealed a surprising lack of faith, especially since it came directly on the heels of God's call and promise to him (Gen 12:1–9). God had instructed Abram to go "to the land that I will show you" (Gen 12:1), promising that the land would belong to him and his descendants (Gen 12:7). Given God's recent promise, Abram should have had more confidence.

Once in Egypt, Abram further demonstrated a lack of faith by instructing Sarai to pretend to be his sister—a decision spurred by Abram's fear of Pharaoh. Despite this, God remained true to his promise and carried Abram and Sarai through Egypt unscathed.

Shortly after this story, Abram's faith was again tested by trial (Gen 13:2–7). While Abram failed the early tests in Egypt, he acted selflessly later, allowing Lot to choose the best area of land. The pairing of these two stories develops a fuller picture of Abram's faith journey: He had both successes and failures when attempting to follow God's will. Together, these stories teach us that although our faith might not be perfect, God's continued faithfulness to us is.

## A CLOSER LOOK

While the main thrust of Genesis 12:10–20 makes sense—Abram chose to travel to Egypt to avoid famine—several aspects of the account raise more questions than answers. What rumors about the Egyptians and foreign women led Abram to fear for his life? While travelers in the ancient world were vulnerable to bandits and forms of discrimination or nationalism, why did Abram feel less safe among the Egyptians than among the Canaanites? What led Abram to suspect that the Egyptians might take advantage of him and his wife, or that they would take Sarai from him? And why didn't Abram, a patriarch of faith, stop and ask God what he should do?

While the details of Genesis 12:10–20 are sparse, they establish a parallel between Abram's later actions and those of his son, Isaac. After arriving in Egypt, Abram told Sarai to identify herself as his sister so the Egyptians, who may have wanted to take her as a wife, wouldn't murder him. He did this again when he and Sarai were in the territory of Abimelech, king of Gerar (Gen 20:1–18; see Chapter 7). Isaac also did nearly the same thing in Gerar (Gen 26:6–11). These parallel accounts establish a pattern in which the patriarch visited a foreign land with his wife and passed her off as his sister to avoid potential harm. In each case, the foreign ruler responded by taking the matriarch into his household (i.e., harem). When the ruse came to light, the ruler sent the patriarch away with his wife and property. In each account, the patriarch acted out of fear, not faith.

> **Quick Bit:** The Hebrew word *gur* (often translated "sojourn" or "dwell") indicates that Abram temporarily emigrated from Canaan to Egypt. He would live in Egypt as an outsider—a stranger dependent on the good will of the locals for his safety and prosperity. In a sense, the use of this word indicates that Abram had considered Canaan his new permanent home, but he was forced by circumstances to temporarily leave.

On some level, Abram's lack of faith was driven by the overwhelming instinct of self-preservation: He didn't want to die. This also manifested as a lack of concern for Sarai. Abram persuaded her to participate in his deception, claiming that he would be killed if she did not. He failed to recognize that because of their ploy, an Egyptian would take her as his wife. Abram's concern for his own survival blinded him to the issues of Sarai's purity and protection.

On another level, though, Abram's actions can be understood as an attempt to preserve the future promised in Genesis 12:2–3. In this light, Abram's focus on his survival reflects a concern to neutralize threats against the fulfillment of God's promise. How could a dead man father a great nation? This episode (and the parallel account of Gen 20) presents Abram struggling with fear—the fear of losing God's promised inheritance. Such fears reflect his humanity: even though God himself had promised him an inheritance and blessing, flashes of doubt and fear plagued him, calling into question his claims of faith.

The story never attempts to defend Abram's actions. Apart from the reference to Sarai's beauty, the account likewise fails to explain why the Egyptians might have wanted to take Sarai and kill Abram. Sarai would have been about 65 years old at this time, making her an unlikely prospect for childbearing. A marriage for political alliance would have also been unlikely since Pharaoh stood to gain nothing from a marriage-based alliance with Abram.

Considering what the story does *not* explicitly say raises even more questions. Sarai was taken into Pharaoh's house (Gen 12:15) and joined his harem (Gen 12:19). Pharaoh's statement that he took her as a wife likely meant that their union was consummated. The consummation may have caused the affliction that later plagued Pharaoh's household. If so, God punished Pharaoh for committing adultery with Abram's wife. When Abram turned to this ruse again in Genesis 20 (see Chapter 7), the story specifically tells us that Sarai was not violated by Abimelech, though his household was unable to bear children until Abram's wife was restored (Gen 20:17). But again, the account of Genesis 12 leaves these kinds of questions unanswered.

> **Quick Bit:** The Hebrew word *naga'* means "to touch," "strike," or "afflict with a plague." Hebrew uses noun and verb forms of the same basic word in tandem. Genesis 12:17 literally says, "And Yahweh afflicted Pharaoh and his household with great afflictions." English translations rarely draw out this feature of the language since it appears redundant in English. Both "afflicted" and "afflictions" are variations of the same basic word. Unfortunately, the word is fairly generic and gives no real clue about the nature of Pharaoh's punishment. However, the context suggests some type of disease.

Upon realizing that the people in his palace were experiencing affliction because he had taken Sarai as his wife, Pharaoh summoned Abram, protested his deceptive actions, and sent him away with Sarai—a terse conclusion to an already unembellished account (Gen 12:18–20). Abram didn't answer Pharaoh's questions; he never explained himself. However, the pattern of these types of narratives suggests that all this was a result of Abram attempting to find some way to survive—either out of fear or out of a misplaced effort to fulfill God's promise to him.

Ultimately, God preserved Abram and faithfully kept his promise despite Abram's seemingly impossible choice—death in Canaan or death in Egypt—and his poor decisions. As we read these accounts, we can recognize times in our own lives when the choices we make seem to lead us off track and away from God. And yet, in such cases, God is still present and able to bring us through any circumstance. He is faithful to his promise.

# THROUGHOUT THE BIBLE

Later in the Bible, most of the attention on Abram focuses on his faithfulness—his obedience to God's calling and acceptance of God's covenant. The story of Genesis 12 emphasizes how God remained faithful to Abram and allowed him to choose his own path; regardless of his choice—Egypt or Canaan—God would have protected Abram and kept the promise to make him a great nation.

A number of psalms recount God's provision to the patriarchs and offer poetic summaries of Israel's history. In one of these, Psalm 105, the psalm calls on the audience to "sing praises" to God and remember his "wonderful works" (Psa 105:2–5). The rest of the psalm recounts God's faithfulness to Abram, Isaac, and Jacob—along with the Israelite nation—for bringing them out of Egypt in the exodus. The psalm emphasizes God's protection of his people and his faithfulness to his promises.

In particular, Psalm 105:12–15 seems to allude to the story of Genesis 12:10-20 and others like it from the lives of the patriarchs. The passage speaks of God's protection of the patriarchs as they wandered as "sojourners ... among the nations" (Psa 105:12-13). Here, the Hebrew word for "sojourners" is the same word used in Genesis 12:10 (Hebrew *gur*). Psalm 105:14 says that God "allowed no one to oppress them," and that "he rebuked kings on account of them." Later, when the psalm recounts how God delivered Israel from Egypt in the exodus, it describes God's motivation in terms of remembrance: "he remembered his holy promise and he remembered Abraham, his servant" (Psa 105:42). God's faithfulness to his promise is central. The episode in which God saved Abram and brought him safely out of Egypt foreshadows his later deliverance of Israel—Abram's descendants—who he brought safely out of Egypt for Abram's sake.

The relationship between these two events may also be alluded to in Isaiah 29:22, where God is identified as the one "who redeemed Abraham." In Genesis 12, God directly redeemed Abram and his household from Egypt. In the exodus account, God redeemed "Abraham" collectively— by redeeming his descendants—when he brought Israel out of Egypt. Later biblical authors used the exodus account as an example of God's faithfulness. God has a special concern for his people and is always in control of their fate. No matter what happens, he faithfully keeps his promises to them.

## BEYOND THE BIBLE

Ancient authors reading the story of Genesis 12:10–20 considered the same questions we've raised—why Abram traveled to Egypt, whether he disobeyed God, why he lied about Sarai, and whether he had a lapse of faith. This story from Abram's life is retold and expanded in one of the Dead Sea Scrolls called the *Genesis Apocryphon*.[3] Written around the first century BC, the *Genesis Apocryphon* is an ancient commentary on the book of Genesis since it contains rewritings of, and expansions upon, its stories. These expansions reflect on the same questions and concerns we're raised about this passage. Like us, the writer of the *Genesis Apocryphon* wrestled with the conflict between Abram's faith and his actions.

> **Quick Bit:** The *Genesis Apocryphon* was one of the first Dead Sea Scrolls discovered in 1947. It was written around the first century BC and contains rewritings of and expansions to the stories of Genesis that serve as a type of commentary.

The expansions also demonstrate the importance of storytelling in both ancient Jewish culture and our own. Storytelling helps us connect our experiences with those of others—even to people we never knew. Telling family stories helps keep the memory and legacy of loved ones alive. Such stories can convey the character of a beloved aunt or grandfather, providing younger generations with models of character and faith to emulate.

To understand the role of storytelling in ancient Jewish culture, imagine you have such a model of character in your family story. You might draw on the stories you know about this person and retell those stories to others. If the specifics of a particular anecdote became difficult to recall, you might easily find yourself *filling in the details* based on how you thought this person would have acted, based on your knowledge of this person's character. Ancient authors did exactly this when writing commentary on Scripture. In the case of Abram, as they read and then retold the biblical account of their ancestor, the lack of detail prompted them to *fill in the details* based on their sense of how Abram would have acted in certain situations.

In response to the many unresolved questions in Genesis 12—the ones we raised in "A Closer Look"—the author of the *Genesis Apocryphon* imaginatively answered them based on his sense of Abram's character. Troubled by the depiction of a conflicted Abram who wavered in the face of God's promise, he retold the story in a way that exonerated Abram's character. The author explained that Abram traveled to Egypt because he had heard about their grain surplus. Along the way, he had a dream—presumably from God—that vividly depicted the couple's fate. In the dream, Sarai lied to protect her husband in order to spare his life. Upon waking, Abram told Sarai about the dream, and she agreed to call him her brother rather than her husband:

> I, Abram, dreamt a dream, on the night of my entry into Egypt. And in my dream I saw a cedar and a palm tree. Some men arrived intending to cut and uproot the cedar, and to leave the palm tree by itself. But the palm tree shouted and said, 'Do not hew down the cedar, because we are from one root.' And the cedar was saved thanks to the palm tree.

The writer justified Abram's fear that the Egyptians would take Sarai by adding a detailed section extolling Sarai's unparalleled beauty. The account states, "Above all women her beauty stands out; her loveliness is far above them all. And with all this beauty there is in her great wisdom. And everything she does with her hands is perfect." The *Genesis Apocryphon* then recounts Abram's extreme grief over losing her. He petitioned God to protect her from sexual defilement, and God sent an afflicting spirit on Pharaoh's household. One of Pharaoh's servants saw Abram in a dream and asked him to come and pray for Pharaoh since none of the wizards or healers of Egypt could cure him. Only then did Pharaoh learn the reason behind his suffering. Afterward, he sent Sarai back to Abram with the promise that he did not consummate his relationship with her.

In this way, the author exonerated both Abram and Sarai by filling in specific details left out of the biblical story. Abram was upset that Sarai was taken, though the biblical story records only that he profited financially (Gen 12:16). Sarai was not sexually violated by Pharaoh, though the biblical story is ambiguous on this point. God informed Pharaoh's household that Abram and Sarai were the cause of their affliction through a dream.

The author of the *Genesis Apocryphon* salvaged Abram's reputation as an exemplar of faith, obedience, and righteousness, but the less-detailed biblical story provides a much more human picture of Abram's struggle between faith and fear. As we look for biblical examples to emulate, the realization that even biblical heroes of faith struggled with doubt should encourage us as we walk in our own journey of faith. Even though we may fail God, he will not fail us.

## APPLICATION

The story of Abram's decision to go to Egypt rather than remain in Canaan raises several themes for those of us who, like Abram, try to live as followers of God. It reminds us that even the heroes of our faith sometimes allowed themselves to be moved by circumstance rather than conviction. And Abram was certainly a hero; he occupies a position of prominence in Hebrews 11 as one of the "cloud of witnesses" whose faith serves as an example to later generations.

Not surprisingly, there is no mention of the events of Genesis 12:10–20 in Hebrews 11. In its portrait of Abram as a man of faith, Abram's decision to go to Egypt rather than remain in Canaan does not even figure as a distant memory—only his commendable actions remain: "By faith Abraham, when he was called, obeyed to go out to a place that he was going to receive as an inheritance, and he went out, not knowing where he was going ... For he was expecting the city that has foundations, whose architect and builder is God" (Heb 11:8, 10).

Considering Hebrews 11 in light of Genesis 12 reminds us that God's faithfulness accompanies our efforts to be faithful. As with Abram, God's promise to finish the work he began in us cannot be deterred by our mistakes and shortcomings. God's faithfulness to us, guaranteed by his grace, will carry us through until the day of Jesus Christ (Phil 1:6).

Living in response to God's call requires that we continually purge ourselves of self-centeredness—or "self-preservation," as in Abram's case. But God's faithfulness to us ensures that even when we find ourselves off course—whether because of a decision made in fear or a sin that has overcome us—his grace will guide us back to his will. For us, the promise God made to Abram finds its full realization in Christ (Gal 3:16). Through Christ, we not only become recipients of God's promise to Abram, we also become heirs of the faithfulness God exhibited toward him. We can be thankful, then, that God's perfect promises are not dependent on our perfect faith. Instead, God's promises secure the perfection of our faith through the redeeming work of his Son (Heb 12:2).

# DISCUSSION

## A Closer Look

1. Reflect on a time when you, like Abram, had doubts about God's plan for your life. Were you tempted to take matters into your own hands without seeking God? Later, were you able to see how God brought you through, even though you thought you'd been left on your own?

_____

_____

2. Reflect on times when you, like Sarai, were carried along by someone else's decision. Did you fear that they were leading you into a bad situation, or did you have faith in their leadership? Discuss how the drive for self-preservation can sometimes cloud our judgment and obscure our view of God's promises.

_____

_____

## Throughout the Bible

1. Read through Psalm 105. How does the psalmist describe God's faithfulness? In what ways can you see God's faithfulness in your life? How can recalling God's faithful deeds of the past (as in Psa 105) strengthen your resolve about his ability to direct your future?

_____

_____

2. Abram's mistakes are not referred to later in Scripture—only his obedience and faith. What does that say to you about God's character? How does this understanding affect your view of God? How does it affect your own faith?

_____

_____

**Beyond the Bible**

1. Think of a Christian or family member who has profoundly affected your life. What about them do you try to emulate? Since Jesus is our supreme model of righteousness and obedience, what are some of the characteristics in his life that you would like to imitate?

_____

_____

_____

2. What character(s) from the Bible do you most identify with? How do biblical characters inspire you to live more righteously or encourage you in your daily walk with God?

_____

_____

_____

**Application**

1. What currently represents "Canaan" for you in your life? What represents "Egypt"? How do you think God wants you to respond to the "Canaan" and "Egypt" in your life? How can you support each other in your resolve to remain in your "Canaan"?

_____

_____

_____

2. How does the knowledge of God's faithfulness and grace give you hope after a "trip to Egypt"? How does a passage like 1 John 1:9 foster this hope?

_____

_____

_____

## CHAPTER 3

# ACTIVE FAITH

*Read Genesis 14:1–24.*

## SETTING THE STAGE

**Theme.** As believers, our walk with God should affect those around us. Our decisions and actions should visibly reflect the commitment we've made as followers of Christ. In the story of Genesis 14:1–24, Abram showed remarkable faith in the wake of failure, and people around him noticed. Comparing Abram's actions to our own might cause us to wonder: Is our faith visible to those around us? Do we adequately testify to God's continuing work in our lives?

Previously, Abram cowered in the face of a difficult circumstance (Gen 12:10-20), despite God's earlier promise of blessing (Gen 12:2-3). He chose to act deceptively, and as a result, God afflicted Pharaoh and his household (Gen 12:17-19). Genesis 14 presents a different side of Abram. Instead of fleeing from danger, Abram displayed remarkable courage and faith. And this time, his actions brought blessing, rather than affliction, to the nations around him—marking the beginning of God's fulfillment of his promise (see Gen 12:3).

**Literary Context.** Genesis 14 is unique among the many stories of Abram's life in that it includes a focus on international events that is largely absent from the rest of the narrative. The account opens with, "in the days of Amraphel, the king of Shinar" (Gen 14:1)—the only time such historical placement is included in Abram's story—and describes the conflicts of several Mesopotamian kings. Genesis 14 also uniquely portrays Abram as a mighty warrior and military leader rather than a wealthy shepherd. This chapter also includes the only appearance of the enigmatic priest-king, Melchizedek, who blessed Abram and received a tithe from him. Despite his brief appearance, Melchizedek became a prominent figure in later biblical interpretation (see the "Throughout the Bible" section).

Previously, Abram and Lot had grown in wealth to the point that the land could not support them, so they split up (Gen 13:2–7). Abram allowed Lot first choice of land; Lot took the best for himself, selecting the Jordan Valley near the city of Sodom (Gen 13:8–13). After this separation, God spoke again to Abram, repeating the original promise that he would give Canaan to Abram's descendants (Gen 13:14–15; see 12:7). God expanded the promise by adding that Abram's descendants would be as numerous as the dust of the earth (Gen 13:16). At the conclusion of chapter 13, Abram had settled in the promised land (Gen 13:18).

In Genesis 14, Lot had fallen into trouble. In choosing to live near Sodom, Lot exposed himself to international conflicts and became the captive of warring Mesopotamian kings (Gen 14:12). The full effect of Lot's decision becomes evident later with God's destruction of Sodom (see Gen 19). Both here and in Genesis 19, Abram saved Lot. Here, Abram intervened directly, defeating the Mesopotamian kings and freeing his nephew (Gen 14:14–16). Later, he interceded on behalf of Lot, asking God to spare Sodom. God still destroyed Sodom, but he remembered Abram's intercession and enabled Lot to escape destruction (Gen 19:29).

As we will see, the events of Genesis 14 show God's first steps in fulfilling his promise to Abram (see Gen 12:1–3). Abram's interaction with the kings in Genesis 14 demonstrates how he would serve as a "blessing" to others (Gen 12:2) and how God would "bless those who bless" him and curse "those who curse" him (Gen 12:3). In defeating the invading kings, Abram protected the land of Canaan, rescued Lot, and restored the possessions of Sodom and Gomorrah. In this account, we see God beginning to use Abram to bring blessing to "all families of the earth" (Gen 12:3).

**Historical & Cultural Background.** As mentioned earlier, Genesis 14 provides more historical information about the time of Abram than any other part of Genesis 12–25. Foreign kings are rarely identified in the narrative of Abram's life (one exception is Abimelech, king of Gerar; see Gen 20). Here, however, the account includes the names of several foreign kings.

The kings of Genesis 14:1 came from the region of Mesopotamia. The first king, Amraphel, whose identity is unknown, came from Shinar, which likely refers to Babylon (see Gen 11:2). The name of the second king, Arioch, may be related to a similar name that appears in the Mari texts (18th century BC tablets found in Syria). His city, Ellasar, probably corresponds with Assur or Assyria. The third king, Chedorlaomer (or Kedorlaomer), was the leader of the alliance. While no Elamite records with this name have been discovered, it is closely related to the Elamite term for "servant," which indicates that it is of Elamite origin. The name of the fourth king, Tidal, may be related to that of the Hittite king Tudhaliya. His region, Goiim, may be related to the Hebrew word for "nations" and simply indicate that Tidal was a "king of peoples." If Goiim refers to a specific place, the location is unknown (see Josh 12:23).

> **Quick Bit:** Chedorlaomer, the leader of the Mesopotamian kings, ruled over the Elamite kingdom, which was located east of Babylon (modern-day Iran). During the Awan Dynasty (2400–2100 BC), Elam's influence grew even as it was under Akkadian rule. Elam expanded militarily during the Simashki Dynasty (2100–1900 BC), sacking Ur and exerting greater influence. The Babylonian king Hammurabi defeated Elam around 1760 BC.

None of the kings of Genesis 14:2 appear outside of the Bible. The names of the kings of Sodom and Gomorrah—Bera and Birsha—may simply be expressions of wordplay, as both begin with the letter b- and are respectively followed by the words for "evil" (*ra'*) and "wicked" (*rasha'*). The exact location of the cities in this verse, especially Sodom and Gomorrah, is disputed. All were likely located around the Dead Sea (the "sea of salt" in Gen 14:3).[1]

As they traveled toward Sodom, the Mesopotamian kings defeated several different people groups (Gen 14:5–7). The identity of these defeated groups shows the extent of the alliance's military strength. The first set—the Rephaim, Zuzim, and Emim—were known as giant clans (see Deut 2:10–11, 20–21). The Horites, while not specifically identified as giants, were often associated with these other clans (Deut 2:12, 22). The Mesopotamian kings must have had mighty armies to be able to defeat these groups. When we recognize these kings' military power, Abram's pursuit and defeat of them becomes even more remarkable.

Ultimately, Abram acted with courageous faith, providing God the opportunity to demonstrate his power and glory by delivering Abram's enemies "into [his] hand" (Gen 14:20).

## A CLOSER LOOK

The most unusual event of Genesis 14 is Abram's visit with Melchizedek. As Abram returned from miraculously defeating the Mesopotamian kings, he was met by the king of Sodom and Melchizedek, the king of Salem. Melchizedek appeared without introduction or explanation and provided bread and wine for Abram and the returning warriors (compare 2 Sam 16:1–2). Who is the strange figure? Why did he bless Abram, and why did Abram give him a tenth of the spoil?

The name Melchizedek (*malki-tsedeq*) likely means "my king is righteous" or "righteous king," which indicates his function at this point in the narrative. Abram had just exercised courageous faith, defeating a powerful army despite overwhelming odds. As the "righteous king," Melchizedek personified righteousness itself and appeared as a royal figure to bless Abram and recognize his triumph.

Melchizedek is also called the "king of Salem," a city traditionally associated with Jerusalem. Psalm 76:2 places Salem in parallel with Zion, the location of God's temple. Some regard "Salem" as an abbreviation of "Jerusalem." Others, however, argue that it was not customary for names to be abbreviated in this manner, suggesting that Salem instead refers to the city of Shechem.[2] Supporters of this view also appeal to Genesis 33:18, which says, "Jacob came safely to the city of Shechem." There, the Hebrew word for "safely" is the same word used for "Salem" in Genesis 14:18. Given this, Genesis 33:18 can be rendered as, "Jacob came to Salem, the city of Shechem." Others believe that Salem is used figuratively rather than to indicate a specific city. The word "Salem" is closely related to the Hebrew word *shalom*, meaning "peace." If this figurative sense was intended, then the text portrays Melchizedek as a "king of peace" as well as a "king of righteousness" (see Heb 7:2).

The story also describes Melchizedek as "the priest of God Most High" (Gen 14:18). Some believe that the title "God Most High" (*el elyon*) represents the name of a Canaanite deity[3]; both *El* and *Elyon* were the names of Canaanite deities, making it possible that *el elyon* is a conflation of the two names. Given the context of Genesis 14, however, this is unlikely. Abram specifically identified "God Most High" as Yahweh—his God (Gen 14:22). The nature of Melchizedek's blessing also indicates that "God Most High" refers to Abram's God, not another deity (Gen 14:19-20).

**Quick Bit:** While the term *elyon* occurs most frequently by itself, it is often seen in parallel with *el* or *elohim*. For example, Psalm 46:4 places "the dwellings of the Most High (*elyon*)" in parallel with "the city of God (*elohim*)." *Elyon* also appears with Yahweh (often translated "Lord") in Psalm 47:2, a verse that emphasizes God's sovereign kingship.

As a title for God, *el elyon* occurs only one other time in this exact form in the Bible (Psa 78:35). On its own, *elyon* emphasizes God's supremacy as ruler and judge over the earth. This emphasis of *elyon* as a name for God certainly aligns with Melchizedek's portrayal of him; as the ruler and judge over all the earth, God's sovereignty extended over the Mesopotamian kings. Melchizedek recognized this and attributed Abram's victory to the "God Most High" (compare Psa 47:2-3). Melchizedek also upheld God as the "Possessor" or "Maker" of heaven and earth, emphasizing God's sovereignty over all of creation (Gen 14:19).

Melchizedek's blessing illustrates the beginning of God's fulfillment of his promise to Abram (Gen 14:19-20). In defeating the Mesopotamian kings, Abram secured the safety of the land and its inhabitants, blessing the nations around him. Melchizedek's recognition and blessing of Abram shows that God had begun to make Abram's name great and bless others as a result (Gen 12:2-3).

Abram responded to Melchizedek's blessing by giving him one-tenth of his spoil. This action blessed Melchizedek and illustrates the initial fulfillment of God's promise that "I will bless those who bless you" (Gen 12:3). And yet, Abram's tithe to Melchizedek has even deeper significance: In giving him one-tenth, Abram recognized Melchizedek's priesthood. Abram's action legitimized the later legal requirement of tithing to support the Levitical priesthood (see Num 18:21-32; Lev 27:30-33). Abram received a priestly blessing and responded in kind; as "father of the nation, [he] set an example for all his descendants to follow."[4]

After Abram and Melchizedek exchanged blessings, the king of Sodom "cursed" Abram and demanded that Abram give him his due and take his deserved spoil (Gen 14:21). Abram wisely distanced himself from the king by refusing to comply (Gen 14:22-24). Although he disassociated himself from the king of Sodom and his territory there, Abram later appealed to God to spare Sodom, again fulfilling his promised role to be a blessing to all nations (see Gen 18:16-33).

Genesis 14 portrays Abram as a person living faithfully within God's promises. Abram's actions showed that he had confidence and faith in God's protection. In contrast to Genesis 12:10-20, Abram did not act out of fear or self-preservation; rather, he swiftly and courageously rescued Lot, trusting that God's promise to make him a great nation would guarantee him success in defeating kings and emperors.

## THROUGHOUT THE BIBLE

Melchizedek's brief and mysterious appearance in Genesis 14 led later biblical writers to expand on his relevance and role. Psalm 110 contains the only other mention of him in the OT. While describing the future success of King David, this psalm includes God's pronouncement, "You are a priest forever according to the manner of Melchizedek" (Psa 110:4). The NT authors understood this as a reference to a future "Son of David" or messianic figure, and Jesus understood his identity in light of this psalm (Matt 22:41-45; Mark 12:35-37; Luke 20:41-44; Acts 2:33-36).

The book of Hebrews expands on this tradition by comparing the priesthoods of Melchizedek and Levi (the priestly tribe responsible for offering sacrifices and caring for Israel's temple; see Num 18; Deut 18), arguing that Melchizedek's priesthood is superior to Levi's. Referring to Abram's tithe in Genesis 14:20, Hebrews claims that because Levi was Abram's descendant, he also participated in Abram's tithe to Melchizedek in Genesis 14 (see Heb 7:9). In doing so, Levi likewise acknowledged the superiority of Melchizedek's priesthood.

In keeping with the overarching theme of the book—the superiority of Christ over all things—Hebrews continues to show that Jesus' priesthood is like Melchizedek's and, by extension, superior to Levi's. The text calls Melchizedek a king and a priest (Heb 7:1) and asserts that Jesus is like him, "according to the order of Melchizedek" (Heb 7:17; see also 5:6, 10; 6:20). Since Jesus is a descendant of David, he is from the royal or kingly tribe of Judah. Unlike the Levites, who were priests because of their genealogy, Jesus was declared to be a priest by God (see Heb 7:16–17). So, like Melchizedek, he is a priest-king. Hebrews 7:2 also states that "Melchizedek, king of Salem" means "king of righteous, king of peace." In this way, too, Jesus—the righteous king who brings peace—is like Melchizedek.

> **Quick Bit:** Christ's priesthood is also superior to the Levites because their priesthood was temporary. Once Israel's temple was destroyed in AD 70, the Levites no longer had any services to perform. But Jesus' priesthood lasts forever.

The nature of Jesus' sacrifice is also everlasting. The Levites' sacrifices could never completely remove sin (see Heb 7:18–19; 10:11), but Jesus' death and resurrection dealt with sin in a final, permanent way (see Heb 7:27). He also intercedes for us, making forgiveness and reconciliation with God possible (see Heb 7:25). A priest in the OT could never accomplish this.

In the life of Abram, Melchizedek is a minor character with seemingly little importance. He enters the story and exits three verses later (Gen 14:18–20). But when viewed throughout the Bible, he takes on far greater relevance. His priesthood provides a means of understanding Jesus' priesthood, anticipating in the OT what becomes fulfilled in the person of Christ.

## BEYOND THE BIBLE

It may seem strange to us that the author of Hebrews selected Melchizedek for his argument as opposed to another kingly or priestly figure. But by looking at texts outside of the Bible, we can see that Melchizedek had become an important figure in first-century Judaism. Since much of the NT was written at this time, Melchizedek was a natural choice.

Ancient writers were fascinated with Melchizedek. Josephus, a first-century Roman Jewish historian, described him as the founder of Jerusalem who built the first temple there (Josephus, *Wars of the Jews* 6.438). Later Jewish interpreters identified Melchizedek as Shem, the son of Noah (see *Targum Neofiti* and Babylonian Talmud 32B).

> **Quick Bit:** The Dead Sea Scrolls are a collection of ancient manuscripts discovered in 1947. While looking for a lost sheep, a nomadic shepherd threw a rock into a cave and heard the sound of pottery shattering. What he found turned out to be the most significant archaeological discovery of the modern area. The scrolls had been stored in 11 caves throughout the Judaean desert, with the largest concentration discovered near the Dead Sea. They contain biblical and non-biblical manuscripts and our oldest existing copies of the OT.

Melchizedek also figures prominently in the Dead Sea Scrolls. One scroll from the first century BC illuminates the tradition of Melchizedek and shows how his role was understood. Known as the "Melchizedek Scroll" (11QMelch or 11Q13), it portrays Melchizedek as a heavenly messianic figure. In the text, Melchizedek executed judgment on Belial (a term for Satan) as well as the "holy ones of God" at the end of days. Strikingly, the scroll describes Melchizedek with language normally reserved for God: "And *your* Elohim is Melchizedek, who will save them from the hand of Belial (Satan)."[5] It also quotes several psalms that speak of God's judgment and applies them to Melchizedek. For example:

> For this is the moment of the Year of Grace for Melchizedek. And he will, by his strength, judge the holy ones of God, executing judgment as it is written concerning him in the Songs of David, who said, Elohim *has taken his place in the divine council; in the midst of the gods he holds judgment* [Psalms 82:1]. And it was concerning him that he said, (Let the assembly of the peoples) *return to the height above them; El (god) will judge the peoples* [Psalms 7:7–8].[6]

The "Melchizedek Scroll" also portrays Melchizedek as a messianic priestly figure. Citing Isaiah 61:1, the scroll says that Melchizedek will proclaim liberty to the captives, "forgiving them the wrong-doings of all their iniquities."[7] In casting him as a redeeming priest and judge, this scroll demonstrates how Jews during the time of Christ understood Melchizedek; he had become a more prominent figure than one would expect from reading only Genesis 14 and Psalm 110. While the book of Hebrews understands Melchizedek differently than the "Melchizedek Scroll," the presence of this tradition helps explain why the author of Hebrews would use this relatively minor character to explain Jesus' messianic priesthood.

# APPLICATION

As followers of Christ, we strive to live in a way that visibly attests to the work of God in our lives. Yet it's easy to feel timid or reluctant about displaying our faith—especially if we've failed before. Abram knew what it was like to fail in trusting God fully. In Genesis 12, he acted out of fear and self-preservation in the face of danger instead of trusting in God's promise (Gen 12:10–20). Yet God remained faithful to him. In Genesis 14, when Abram learned that his nephew was in danger, he didn't hesitate to act. Emboldened by God's promise, Abram confidently set his eyes on the armies of the Mesopotamian kings, and with his band of trained men, he took down an army of giants.

Our past failures or lapses of faith do not prevent God from using us to accomplish great things, whether in witnessing to his work in our lives or defeating armies of giants (see Psa 118:6; Rom 8:31). Abram's life shows us that God can and will use us *despite* our weaknesses and failures (see 1 Cor 1:26–31). This encourages us, like the Apostle Paul, to recognize that God's grace is sufficient and that his power is made evident through our weakness (2 Cor 12:9).

In Colossians 3:17, Paul wrote, "whatever you do, in word or deed, do everything in the name of the Lord Jesus" (ESV). Paul recognized that when we live out our faith, others notice—and they benefit from our efforts. This was true in Abram's life: The Canaanite priest-king Melchizedek recognized Abram's courage and, more importantly, God's hand in Abram's victory. Our faith should not only affect us, it should affect those around us as we respond to God's call to live as disciples of Christ (see Col 3:12–15).

# DISCUSSION

## A Closer Look

1. Think of a situation that required you to act in faith. How did you respond? How could you see God's hand in your decisions?

_____

_____

_____

2. How does your faith affect those around you? Would you consider yourself a "blessing" to others?

_____

_____

_____

## Throughout the Bible

1. Read Hebrews 7. How does the writer compare Melchizedek to Christ? How does Christ's priesthood compare with the Levitical priesthood? How should Christ's "once for all" (Heb 7:27) sacrifice affect how we live?

_____

_____

_____

2. Melchizedek's priesthood prepares NT readers for understanding Jesus' priesthood. Can you think of other times when a person or event in the OT helps us understand something about Christ?

_____

_____

_____

## Beyond the Bible

1. God used the minor character of Melchizedek to convey truths that affect his eternal plan of salvation for humanity. What other biblical examples can you think of where God used seemingly insignificant people or events to convey eternal truths? What does this say about the nature of God and how he relates to his creation?

2. Where else have you found references to Jesus in the OT? What does each one tell you about God's plan of salvation?

## Application

1. Read 1 Corinthians 1:26–31 and 2 Corinthians 12:9–10. How does Paul describe our weakness compared to God's strength? How does this encourage you to rely on the Lord?

2. How can you show God's love to others by living faithfully? How does putting to death "what is earthly" and putting on a new being affect how you relate to others (see Col 3:5–17)?

## CHAPTER 4

# DEALING WITH DOUBT

*Read Genesis 15:1–21; 16:1–15.*

## SETTING THE STAGE

**Theme.** It's only natural to have doubts after someone has promised us the same thing time and again but hasn't followed through. It can be difficult to maintain patience in the wake of disappointed expectation. Inaction, whether real or perceived, can erode trust and confidence. Eventually, we need an incredible amount of assurance before we can accept that person's word again.

In Genesis 15–16, Abram expressed this kind of doubt regarding God's promise of a son. God's promise remained unfulfilled, and Abram needed new reassurance from God. But even after God provided this reassurance, Abram and Sarai still hesitated to fully trust that he would keep his word. They came up with a plan to overcome Sarai's barrenness and provide Abram with the son he longed for. Ultimately, they looked beyond the promise and took matters into their own hands.

**Literary Context.** The opening verses of Genesis 15 indicate that Abram had lost his sense of confidence. Previously, Abram exhibited great faith in rescuing Lot and defeating several kings in battle (Gen 14:1–16). God recognized this faith and ensured Abram's success, causing him to be victorious (Gen 14:20). Genesis 15 opens with God encouraging Abram to continue trusting in him. God tells Abram, "I am your shield," alluding to Abram's military victory (Gen 15:1). Abram's response, however, reveals a surprising amount of insecurity, especially given his recent battlefield success. Indicating his sense of doubt, Abram reminds God that he is still childless (Gen 15:2).

In earlier chapters, God had repeated his promise to Abram several times in different forms. He had originally promised to make Abram a "great nation" and to make his name great (Gen 12:1–3). He had also promised to give the land of Canaan to Abram's offspring (Gen 12:7). Later, God promised Abram that his offspring would be as numerous as the "dust of the earth" (Gen 13:14–17). However, time had passed, and Abram and Sarai still lacked a child.

This delay caused Abram to doubt. He wondered if perhaps his servant, Eliezer, was supposed to be his heir and inherit the land God had promised him. Abram bluntly explained the problem to God: "Look, you have not given me a descendant" (Gen 15:3). God responded not with rebuke— although this would have been justified—but with reassurance. In repeating the promise yet again, God explicitly stated that Abram's *own* son would be the heir (Gen 15:4). Abram responded by trusting in God (Gen 15:6), and God led Abram in a ritual confirming the covenant promise (Gen 15:9–20).

In Genesis 16, despite God's confirmation, we find Abram again doubting that God would fulfill his promise. Sarai proposed that Abram take her servant, Hagar, and have children with her (Gen 16:2). Abram agreed, and Hagar conceived (Gen 16:3–4). Hagar's pregnancy caused strife between her and Sarai, who sent Hagar away (Gen 16:5–6). God intervened, and Hagar returned to give birth to Ishmael (Gen 16:15).

**Historical & Cultural Background.** Sarai's suggestion that Abram have children through her servant may seem strange to us. However, this was a common solution to infertility in the ancient Near East. According to an Assyrian marriage document from the 19th century BC, if the bride could not provide her husband with offspring, she had to purchase a slave woman for childbearing.[1] An Akkadian tablet from the 15th century BC lists a similar requirement, adding that the children of the slave woman must be given the inheritance and not be sent away:

> Furthermore, Kelim-ninu has been given in marriage to Shennima.
> If Kelim-ninu bears (children), Shennima shall not take another

wife; but if Kelim-ninu does not bear, Kelim-ninu shall acquire a woman of the land of Lullu as wife for Shennima, and Kelim-ninu may not send the offspring away. Any sons that may be born to Shennima from the womb of Kelim-ninu, to (these) sons shall be given [all] the lands (and) buildings of every sort. (Akkadian Legal Tablet [15th Century BC])[2]

Other ancient legal texts include similar stipulations. The Laws of Lipit-Ishtar—a set of Sumerian laws from the 20th century BC—indicate that if a man's wife has not produced children, but the man has a child by a prostitute, that child should be his heir.[3] The Code of Hammurabi, an ancient Babylonian law code, also contains several laws regarding children born by slave women.[4]

The commonality of this practice helps explain why Abram and Sarai turned to Hagar to produce a child. Furthermore, 11 years had passed between the time Abram first received God's promise and the birth of Ishmael.[5] Abram had already waited more than a decade for God to fulfill his word—and yet, Abram's time of waiting was still not over. He was 100 years old when Isaac was born, meaning that he had to wait more than two decades before he had a legitimate heir (Gen 21:5). In Genesis 15–16, Abram's time of waiting on God was not even half over—a key point to remember as we examine these chapters more closely.

## A CLOSER LOOK

In Genesis 15, Abram is more vocal and less deferential to God than in previous chapters. Earlier, Abram had simply accepted God's promise and acted in good faith (Gen 12:1–9), but here, Abram questioned God's plan and sought tangible details. We find Abram voicing his doubts and expressing his need for reassurance (Gen 15:2–3). As one scholar notes, "Throughout the Genesis narratives, when Abraham speaks he gives expression to questions that appear to reveal doubt. On the other hand, when, in the narratives, he is silent, his actions always exhibit faith."[6]

Abram's questions in Genesis 15:2–3 led God to restate that he would provide Abram with offspring as numerous as the stars (Gen 15:5). Following this, the narrative highlights Abram's belief, stating that Abram "believed in Yahweh, and he reckoned it to him as righteousness" (Gen 15:6), almost as if to reiterate this point before Abram questioned God again. God then repeated his initial promise to provide Abram with land (Gen 12:7). Yet instead of expressing belief, Abram replied with hesitation and demanded proof (Gen 15:8). His seemed to doubt not just that he would possess the land, but that God would provide him with descendants to inherit it.

To meet Abram's challenge, God initiated a ritual intended to confirm his covenant promise. He commanded Abram to slaughter five animals—a heifer, a goat, a ram, a turtledove, and a pigeon. Abram did so, dividing the larger animals in half and laying the pieces across from each other.

> **Quick Bit:** In Genesis 15, Abram's special relationship with God is presented in a way that emphasizes his role as a prophet. The chapter opens with the phrase "the word of Yahweh came to Abram in a vision" (Gen 15:1), phrasing found in other prophetic books (Jer 1:2; Ezek 1:3). Abram then received a vision of future events regarding Israel's bondage in Egypt and eventual exodus (Exod 1–12).

He then drifted off into a "deep sleep" (Gen 15:12), during which God revealed that his descendants would experience captivity and slavery before returning to the land of promise. This prophetic insight was meant to reassure Abram by providing specific details of when God's promise would be fulfilled. In emphasizing that God had future plans for Abram's offspring, this vision reassured Abram that God had a long-term plan in place (Gen 15:13–21).

After the prophecy, God confirmed his covenant with Abram by causing a smoking firepot and flaming torch to pass between the pieces of the slaughtered animals (Gen 15:17). Imagery of smoke and fire often accompanies appearances of God in the Bible (e.g., Exod 3:2; 19:18). Here, this imagery is likely intended to foreshadow God's appearance to Israel at Mount Sinai (Deut 4:11). Unlike at Sinai, however, God's covenant with Abram is one-sided: Only God passed through the pieces; he alone took responsibility for fulfilling his promise to Abram.

The covenant ritual was not a sacrifice; rather, it indicated that an agreement had been established and likely alluded to how people in the ancient Near East ratified treaties. Specifically, it was probably intended to be associated with a formal legal grant of the land to Abram. In effect, God used an ancient Near Eastern legal procedure to confirm his commitment to Abram.

> **Quick Bit:** In the ancient Near East, people could ratify a treaty by walking between rows of freshly slaughtered animals. In doing so, both parties acknowledged that if they reneged on the terms of their agreement, they deserved the same fate as the animals. Here, the passing of the firepot and torch between the animal halves indicated God's commitment to his covenant with Abram (Gen 15:17–19).

Despite God's reassurance in Genesis 15, Abram's lingering doubts led him to "listen to the voice of Sarai" (Gen 16:2). Along with the meaning of the covenant ritual, the mention of the 10 people groups occupying Canaan at the end of Genesis 15 likewise suggests that God's covenant was directly connected to the promise of land (Gen 15:19–21). Perhaps Abram felt confident in this part of God's promise but not in his promise of an heir. He may have concluded that God had addressed only one of his concerns.

In Genesis 16, Sarai worked around her infertility by providing Abram with a surrogate mother for his child. Since God's promise up to this point had only specified that Abram would have offspring, not that the offspring would be through Sarai, her actions were reasonable. Sensing that she was the obstacle preventing God's promise from being fulfilled, Sarai offered her maid, Hagar, to Abram as a secondary wife. Hagar's status as Sarai's slave meant that any child born to Hagar would have had the same legal standing as Sarai's child. Abram agreed to Sarai's plan, and Hagar became pregnant. Abram and Sarai likely failed to recognize their plan for what it was: an attempt to hurry the fulfillment of God's promise.

Understanding the meaning of the Hebrew word *zera'* sheds light on Abram and Sarai's use of Hagar in Genesis 16. The word *zera'* literally means "seed" and is used for both plants (Gen 1:11) and animals (Jer 31:27). Often used to refer to human descendants (Gen 3:15; Ruth 4:12), *zera'* can also refer to semen (Lev 18:20). Ancient Israelites believed *zera'* to be the "seed" that produced offspring when "planted" in a woman. Providing Abram with an heir was simply a matter of providing an alternative womb in which to plant his "seed." God had promised him a son, but until now, he had not indicated that it was to be through Sarai.

While we don't learn of God's disapproval of Abram and Sarai's actions until Genesis 17:19, their attempt to influence the outcome of his promise quickly led to unforeseen strife. Hagar's pregnancy became a source of contempt between her and Sarai. Hagar likely felt proud that she conceived, and Sarai was jealous of her success. Hagar unwisely developed an overconfident attitude toward Sarai. While the plan was Sarai's idea, Sarai blamed Abram for the outcome. After Abram gave Sarai free rein to discipline Hagar, Sarai treated Hagar so harshly that she ran away.

In the wilderness, an angel appeared to Hagar and convinced her to return to Sarai and Abram. The angel instructed her to name her son Ishmael (meaning "God hears") and promised that he, too, would become a great nation. The angel's command in Genesis 16:9 implied that Hagar could expect divine blessing and assistance, but only if she maintained her connection to Abram. This reaffirmed God's promise that all families of the earth would be blessed through Abram (Gen 12:3).

The angel also revealed that Ishmael's life would be characterized by conflict and hostility, not peaceful blessing (Gen 16:12). In this way, the angel indicated that Ishmael was not the promised son, and his descendants would not inherit the land—this would be reserved for another son. Hagar accepted this and prayed to God before returning to Sarai. She called him the "God of seeing," or "El-Roi" (Gen 16:13), unwittingly affirming what Sarai and Abram had overlooked: God oversees and directs everything, and those who follow him never have any reason to doubt his plan.

## THROUGHOUT THE BIBLE

When NT writers talk about Abram, they tend to focus on his faith and overlook that he sometimes acted out of fear and doubt. With the benefit of hindsight, they could look back on Abram's story and emphasize the acts of faith in his life. Even though the OT covers 25 years of Abram's life before Isaac's birth, NT writers focused on the big picture: God promised

Abram offspring, Abram believed, and Isaac was born. For example, Hebrews 11 summarizes Abram's life in eight verses (Heb 11:8–12, 17–19) and compresses his call, his response of faith, and the birth of Isaac into a five-verse span.

The Apostle Paul frequently draws from Abram's example of faithful obedience when using the OT to preach the gospel. In both Romans 4 and Galatians 3, where he emphasizes the superiority of faith over the law, he appeals to Abram's example and cites Genesis 15:6. As in Hebrews 11, Paul's short summary of Abram's life in Romans 4 focuses on his faith, smoothing out the ups and downs of his life. Paul mentions Abram's faith or belief a total of 12 times in Romans 4 to address this question: Was Abram justified on the basis of his deeds or the basis of his faith?[7] Paul identifies Genesis 15:6 as providing the definitive answer: "And he believed in Yahweh, and he reckoned it to him as righteousness."

Paul's discussion of Abram in Galatians seems especially designed to address those who might have argued that Abram had combined faith with obedience to the law—even though the law hadn't yet been formally given in Abram's time.[8] Paul emphasizes that Abram's faith in God's promise came long before the law and was in no way dependent on the law (Gal 3:17–18). His use of Genesis 15:6 in Galatians 3:6 emphasizes that God makes people righteous on the basis of faith, not works (Gal 3:5–7).

In Galatians 3:16, Paul demonstrates that God's promise to provide Abram with a son was really a promise to one day send his Son, Jesus Christ. To make this point, Paul cites the Genesis references to Abraham's "seed" or "offspring" (Hebrew *zera'*), emphasizing that God used "seed" (singular) rather than "seeds" (plural) when promising descendants to Abraham (e.g., Gen 12:7; 13:16). While Abraham waited 25 years for the initial fulfillment of the promise in the birth of Isaac, the world waited much longer for the ultimate fulfillment of the promise in Christ. God favored Isaac, the child of the promise, over Ishmael, who was "born according to human descent" (Gal 4:23). But Paul also understands the story of Genesis 16 allegorically in that Ishmael represents those who labor under the law, whereas Isaac represents those saved by faith in Christ. Thus Paul uses this part of Abram and Sarai's life to illustrate and preach the gospel. Just as Abram was justified by faith (Gen 15:6), so those who follow Christ are justified by faith, not the law (Gal 3:21–22).

# BEYOND THE BIBLE

The delayed fulfillment of God's promise of a son caused Abram to lament, "A slave born in my house is to be my heir" (Gen 15:3 NRSV). This sorrowful expression led John Chrysostom—an influential leader in the early church—to write, "[Abram's] words reveal the extreme degree of the pain in his soul."[9] Chrysostom's words help bring to light the human dimension of Abram's struggle in the opening of Genesis 15 (Gen 15:2-3). His experience of delay regarding the fulfillment of God's promise caused him to suffer deeply (see Prov 12:13).

> **Quick Bit:** John Chrysostom was one of the church fathers—a group of about 20 influential thinkers and teachers in the first few centuries of the Church. An eloquent preacher, Chrysostom lived during the latter half of the fourth century (ca. AD 344-407) and served as the Bishop of Constantinople.

Yet, as Genesis 15 narrates, God used this opportunity to reaffirm his covenant with Abram. This gracious reaffirmation prompted Chrysostom to conclude, "[Abram] spoke boldly to the Lord, revealed the tumult of his interior thoughts and made no secret of the wound to his spirit. Hence in turn he received instant healing."[10] Chrysostom cast God's response to Abram's "tumult" as an expression of his mercy (Gen 15:4). Mindful of Abram's experience of suffering, God reassured him by rearticulating the promise.

> **Quick Bit:** Ambrose was also one of the church fathers. He lived during roughly the same time as Chrysostom (ca. AD 333-397) and ministered as the Bishop of Milan. He is best known for his reputation as a theologian and a teacher of Augustine.

Still, Abram and Sarai pursued an alternative means of obtaining the son of promise (see Gen 16:2). Another early church figure, Ambrose of Milan, recognized in this episode God's protection of Abram's descendants—the source for the ultimate Son of promise, Jesus Christ. Abram and Sarai intervened in God's plan and, from the human perspective, messed things up. Ambrose asserted that despite this, God intervened to ensure the legitimacy of the Messiah's heritage—that he would be a son of Abram by Sarai:

> But in Isaac, the legitimate son, we can see the one who is the true legitimate Son, the Lord Jesus, of whom at the beginning of the Gospel according to Matthew we read that he is the son of Abraham. (Ambrose, *On Abraham* 1.3.20)[11]

Despite Abram and Sarai's impatience, God displayed his grace and sovereignty by providing them with reassurance and protection. Early Christian teachers like Chrysostom and Ambrose highlighted these themes to encourage the communities they served. We, too, can take refuge in them and trust that God will bring about his promises according to his divinely ordained timing. God's perfect track record for doing what he says provides reassurance in times of delay.

## APPLICATION

God is infinite—he has no beginning or end, and he is not subject to any limitation. We are the exact opposite, which is why it can be difficult for us to wait on him. Yet God, in his grace, understands our limitations and is patient with us. Even when we sense delay and attempt to speed up God's plan, he sovereignly brings about his promises according to his perfect timing.

This part of Abram's story powerfully illustrates this lesson for us. Sensing delay, Abram voiced his concern about not yet having a son (Gen 15:2–3). God met Abram at the point of his need and responded to him in loving, tangible ways. He went to great lengths to provide Abram with the assurance he needed and to make his promise alive to Abram again. He led him out into the starry night and told him, "count the stars if you are able … So shall your offspring be" (Gen 15:5). He had Abram select a set of animals from his flock, slaughter them, and cut them in half to show that he would keep his end of the bargain. And all the while, God spoke words of comfort to his servant.

Yet God's gracious intervention was not enough to quell Abram and Sarai's anxiety because, as described in 2 Peter 3:8, "one day with the Lord is like a thousand years, and a thousand years is like one day." Just as we do when we think we cannot wait on God any longer, they took action on their own and produced an heir for Abram before God's appointed time. Impatient decisions often lead to unforeseen consequences; the actions of Abram and Sarai brought a child into a situation of conflict and discord. Even before his birth, Ishmael was marked as one who would "live in hostility with all his brothers" (Gen 16:12).

When our "thousand years" seem to be without end, God wishes for us to submit to his timing. When our patience is tried, Abram's example helps us recall that "the Lord is not delaying the promise"; rather, he is simply bringing about his plan according to his flawless design (2 Pet 3:9).

# DISCUSSION

## A Closer Look

1. Think about a time when you had doubts about God's plan for you. How did you respond to those doubts? Did you take matters into your own hands? Did you experience anything that reassured you that you were on the right track?

_____

_____

_____

2. Just like Abram, we can experience doubt even as we walk the path of faith. Have you ever doubted God—his existence or his ability to do what he promised? How can understanding the struggles of Abram and Sarai bring light to your own struggles with doubt?

_____

_____

_____

## Throughout the Bible

1. How does Paul's emphasis on faith over works affect how you think about serving others? What is Paul really concerned about?

_____

_____

_____

2. Paul uses the story of Hagar and Sarah to teach something important about God's promises. What lessons has God taught you through someone else's mistake?

_____

_____

## Beyond the Bible

1. Can you think of a time when you've had to wait on God? How did he gracefully sustain you through the process?

_____

_____

_____

2. How does God's character, as revealed in Scripture, reassure you that he'll do exactly what he's said?

_____

_____

_____

## Application

1. Consider the ways God actively reaffirmed his promise to Abram. How do you see God acting in your life to remind you of his promises for you?

_____

_____

_____

2. Think about Abram's experience of having a promise delayed. How does his experience lend perspective to our lives as we wait for the promise of Christ's return? What does Abram's experience teach us as we wait?

_____

_____

_____

## CHAPTER 5

# PROMISING THE IMPOSSIBLE

*Read Genesis 17:1–18:15.*

## SETTING THE STAGE

**Theme.** While it's easy to pay lip service to the idea that God is all powerful, it's much more difficult to consistently live out our faith in ways that recognize God's unlimited ability—his omnipotence. Like other characteristics attributed to God,[1] omnipotence can be a difficult idea to wrap our heads around. The story of Abram and Sarai shows that even the heroes of faith sometimes found it difficult to acknowledge God's power in their lives.

In Genesis 17 and 18, Sarai and Abram struggled to keep their composure when God delivered the seemingly ridiculous news that Sarai—a 90-year-old woman who had been barren her whole life—would give birth to a son. In response to Sarai's laughter of disbelief, God raised the issue of his omnipotence, asking, "Is anything too difficult for Yahweh?" (Gen 18:14). The story goes on to show that "with God all things are possible" (Matt 19:22), even when we have trouble believing it. God eventually made Sarai a mother, demonstrating his ability to bring life from a previously lifeless womb—and he did so despite the couple's doubts.

**Literary Context.** As we've seen, God repeated his promise to Abram several times throughout his life. Each time, God made the promise more specific. He first promised Abram that he would become a "great nation" (Gen 12:1–3) and identified the land that he would give to Abram's offspring (Gen 12:7). Later, he revealed that Abram's descendants would be as numerous as the dust of the earth (Gen 13:14–17). Even later, he made it known that the heir to the promise would be Abram's own son (Gen 15:4) and identified the specific location of the promised land (Gen 15:18–21).

In Genesis 17:1–27, God again reaffirmed his promise to Abram. While most of this promise resembled earlier versions, a few things were new. God stated that kings would be included among Abram's descendants (Gen 17:6, 16) and emphasized that a son birthed by Sarai would inherit the covenant (Gen 17:19). Here, God also changed the names of Abram and Sarai to Abraham and Sarah and established circumcision as the sign of the covenant.

In the chapter that follows, three men visit Abraham on their way to Sodom (Gen 18:1–15). While we are told that "Yahweh appeared to [Abraham]" (Gen 18:1), the chapter does not identify the three men or provide details about their interaction with Abraham (they appear in Gen 18:2). Rather, it focuses on Abraham's hospitality; he invited the men to rest and provided a feast for them (Gen 18:3–8). These men are typically understood as messengers from God or a representation of God himself (see "Beyond the Bible").

**Historical & Cultural Background.** The story of Genesis 18 illustrates the significance of hospitality in the ancient Near East. The Babylonian Talmud says, "Greater value attaches to hospitality ... than receiving the presence of God."[2] Hosts were responsible for protecting their guests as well as providing water (so visitors could wash their feet) and a meal (see Gen 24:32; 43:24; Judg 19:21). They were also expected to care for their guests' animals (see Gen 24:31–32; 43:24).

> **Quick Bit:** The Babylonian Talmud is a rabbinic commentary on the Jewish law written between AD 500 and 600. The Hebrew word *talmud* means "instruction, learning."

The social and cultural significance of hospitality is also evident in the Psalms, which sometimes portray God as a host. Psalm 23 describes the provision and protection that comes with being a guest in the house of Yahweh; it tells how God satisfies the psalmist's hunger by setting a "table" before him and provides him with sanctuary by doing so "in the presence of [his] oppressors" (Psa 23:5-6). Psalm 36:8 likewise describes the refreshment that comes to those who take refuge in God's house.

The Gospel writers also used the role of host in their portrayal of Jesus and his ministry. Jesus practiced hospitality by providing food for the crowds that had been following him (Mark 8:1-9). He also served as a host when washing his disciples' feet; earlier, he had criticized a Pharisee for not providing him with this service (John 13:3-5; see Luke 7:44-47). Understanding ancient Near Eastern hospitality helps us better understand not only Abraham's story, but other biblical passages as well.

## A CLOSER LOOK

Genesis 17 opens by telling us "Abram was ninety-nine years old" when Yahweh appeared to him again (Gen 17:1). Thirteen years had passed since the events of Genesis 15-16 (see Gen 16:16), yet the narrative doesn't focus on this fact. Instead, it simply presents God's reiteration of the promise. This shows that the relationship between the events of Genesis 16 and 17 is more important than *when* the events of each chapter occurred. Previously, Sarai had tried to bring about the fulfillment of God's promise by providing Abram with an heir through Hagar. Here, as we'll see, God affirmed that Sarai herself would bear a son. This particular arrangement of events emphasizes the themes of promise and faith in Abram and Sarai's life.

The chapter begins with God once more interacting directly with Abram, identifying himself as "El-Shaddai" or "God Almighty" (Gen 17:1). In his previous encounters with Abram, God had required very little from him (see Gen 12, 15). Here, God commanded that Abram "walk before me and be blameless," establishing Abram's obedience as a condition of his blessing and covenant (Gen 17:1-2).

God also restated the promise and reinstated the covenant—a course of action required by the events of Genesis 16. The time for fulfillment of the promise was drawing near. God's reassurance to Abram in Genesis 15 had focused on the promise of the land (see Chapter 4, "A Closer Look"). In this reinstatement of the covenant promise, God emphasized that Abram would be the "father of a multitude of nations" (Gen 17:4–5). God had already attempted to give Abram some sense of how numerous his descendants would be, comparing their number to the dust of the earth (Gen 13:16) and the stars of the sky (Gen 15:5). Here, he emphasized that Abram would father not only a "great nation," but a "multitude" of them (Gen 17:4). To underscore this promise, God renamed him Abraham, connecting his new name to the promise that he would father this multitude (Gen 17:5). No longer would Abraham merely be a revered figure; he would become the ancestor to whom many people groups would trace their beginning.

> **Quick Bit:** The name Abram means "Exalted Father." The name Abraham is explained in Genesis 17:5 as meaning "father of a multitude of nations." This meaning for Abraham is probably based on the wordplay between *av* ("father") and the words *raham* and *hamon*, both of which mean "multitude." This name served a daily reminder of Abraham's ultimate destiny.

God then introduced circumcision by commanding Abraham, "you must keep my covenant, you and your offspring after you, throughout their generations" (Gen 17:9). Previously, the covenant simply established that Canaan would belong to Abraham's descendants (Gen 15:18–21). Now, the covenant required obedience to God's command that every male be circumcised. As "a sign of the covenant," circumcision functioned as a symbol—an external act of obedience that testified to an inward faith in God's promise (Gen 17:11). The symbolism of circumcision had a lasting impact on biblical writers (see "Throughout the Bible").

After providing details on circumcision (Gen 17:11–14), God renamed Sarai, calling her Sarah (both names mean "princess"; Gen 17:15). Then, God finally provided Abraham with the essential detail: The promised son would be born through Sarah (Gen 17:16). As if to emphasize the link between his promise to Abraham and his blessing of Sarah, God continued by stating that nations and kings would come through her (Gen 17:16). Stunned by this revelation, Abraham laughed, wondering how an elderly couple could have children (Gen 17:17). He then addressed God, begging him to bless his son, Ishmael, instead (Gen 17:18). But God's plan was set: Isaac would be the son of the promise (Gen 17:19, 21).

After 24 years of waiting on God, Abraham finally received a concrete timeframe: Sarah would have a son within the year (Gen 17:21). With this final assurance in place, Abraham proceeded to circumcise every male in his household, as God commanded (Gen 17:23).

In the scene that follows, Abraham offered hospitality to three divine messengers (Gen 18:1–15), who repeated the promise that Sarah would have a son within the year (Gen 18:10). This episode focuses on Sarah's response to this prophecy: Upon over-hearing their announcement, she laughed in disbelief. While Sarah's reaction is understandable, given her age and lifelong inability to conceive, Yahweh chastised Sarah for her doubt (Gen 18:13). Sarah denied her reaction, likely out of surprise over the scolding and for having the visitor know her thoughts (Gen 18:15).

As the story ends, the sense of immediacy in this selective presentation of events from Abraham's life becomes apparent (Gen 16–18:15). Abram may have patiently waited on God during the 13 years between Genesis 16 and 17. Perhaps he had assumed Ishmael would be his heir and that God had approved of their intervention via Hagar (implied by his reaction in Gen 17:18). Ultimately, however, these stories show that God seems to take delight in performing the impossible.

## THROUGHOUT THE BIBLE

In Genesis 17:9–14, God established circumcision as a tangible sign of his covenant with Abraham. From then on, circumcision became a central part of Israelite religion. Mosaic law required all male children to be circumcised eight days after their birth (Lev 12:3). When the Israelites left Egypt, God instructed Moses to circumcise any foreigners who wanted to join them (Exod 12:48–49). Joshua circumcised the generation born in the wilderness before leading them into Canaan (Josh 5:3–7).

While circumcision served as a physical sign of God's covenant, it was also understood symbolically in the OT. In Deuteronomy 10:16, Moses instructed the Israelites to circumcise their hearts, a command that the prophet Jeremiah later repeated (Jer 4:4). The OT also repeatedly describes the wicked as having an "uncircumcised heart" (Lev 26:41; Jer 9:26; Ezek 44:9).

The biblical writers understood the act of circumcision as conveying the inward reality of a changed heart.

> **Quick Bit:** The Council of Jerusalem was a meeting of the apostolic church leaders that took place around AD 50 (Acts 15:1–29). Its main focus was to decide whether Gentile believers should be required to follow the Mosaic law. The council ultimately decided that Gentile believers were only required to follow certain dietary laws and abstain from sexual immorality (Acts 15:29).

Circumcision was not only important to the Israelites—it also played a major role in the writings of the NT and the self-understanding of the early church. In the first century AD, Jewish believers disagreed about whether Gentile believers needed to be circumcised. Some Jewish believers thought that Gentiles had to be circumcised when they came to faith in Christ (Acts 15:1). Others, inspired by Peter's encounter with the Gentile centurion, Cornelius (Acts 10:34–47), recognized that God gave the Holy Spirit to uncircumcised Gentiles when they believed (see Acts 15:8–11). The issue was definitively settled at the Council of Jerusalem, where the leaders of the early church decided that Gentiles did not need to be circumcised after proclaiming faith in Jesus (Acts 15:1–29).

Despite this decision, false teachers known as Judaizers tried to force Gentile believers to be circumcised (Gal 6:12). Paul spent major portions of his letters addressing this topic. He explained to Roman believers that circumcision does not truly reflect obedience or faithfulness (Rom 2:25–28). Drawing on OT passages like Deuteronomy 10:16 and Jeremiah 4:4, Paul argued that inward circumcision of the heart is more valuable than the physical act (Rom 2:29).

> **Quick Bit:** Judaizers were Jewish believers who tried to force Gentiles in the early church to adopt a Jewish lifestyle. They insisted that Gentile believers be circumcised and follow the Mosaic law. Paul argued against them in his letters, especially Galatians (Gal 2:12–14; 6:12).

Paul also used the life of Abraham to show that circumcision is not necessary for salvation. In Romans 4, he argued that Abraham's faith was the basis of God's promise; circumcision only served as a sign or symbol of God's covenant. Paul based this argument on the progression of the events in Abraham's life (Rom 4:10–11): Abraham received the sign of circumcision later in his life (Gen 17:10–11), after his faith had been credited to him as righteousness (Gen 15:6). Establishing that Abraham was considered righteous before his circumcision, Paul maintained that Abraham is the father of all who believe, whether or not they are circumcised (Rom 4:9, 12).

## BEYOND THE BIBLE

The story of Genesis 18 opens with Yahweh appearing to Abraham (Gen 18:1) and the two speaking with each other (Gen 18:10–14). Yet, we are also told that Abraham waited on three men (Gen 18:2, 9, 16). Who were they? The answer to this question reveals a great deal about how God views his promises and what they mean to the world.

> **Quick Bit:** Josephus (ca. AD 37–100) is best known as a Jewish historian. Prior to his career as a historian, he had a leading role in the Jewish war against Rome. After being captured by the Romans, Josephus gained their favor and was given the freedom to begin his literary career.

The ancient Jewish historian, Josephus, identified these three visitors as angels. Josephus noted that after Sarah had reacted to the news that she would be a mother, "[T]hey no longer disguised themselves but revealed that they were messengers of God and that one of them had been sent to make a disclosure concerning the child."[3] Some ancient interpreters thought that God himself was one of the three visitors. However, Josephus' retelling reflects the attitude of his Roman readers, who may have considered it impossible that the Jewish God—the Creator of the universe— would take on human form and converse with them.

> **Quick Bit:** Philo (ca. 20 BC–AD 50) was a Jewish philosopher, apologist, and commentator on the Hebrew Scriptures. His many works tell us much about the intersection of Greek and Jewish thought during the time of Christ.[4]

But other ancient commentators such as Philo—a Jewish philosopher and interpreter of Scripture—insisted that Abraham met with God himself. Philo wrote, "Inasmuch as he, according to my conception, was the true and living God … thought it fitting that he being present should bestow good gifts by his own power."[5] He asserted that God himself was one of the three visitors, and that he appeared to Abraham to announce that he would have a son the following year.

Philo's view is in agreement with the biblical text; the Jewish name for God, Yahweh, is used of one of the visitors (see Gen 18:1, 13, 17, 20, 22, 26, 33). Rather than send an angel to announce the impending birth of Isaac, God appeared to deliver the message personally. With benefit of hindsight, we now recognize that this "guest appearance" indicates the importance of the covenant—one that would only be realized several centuries later. Jesus the Messiah, the promised Son of God and a descendant of Abraham, is the ultimate fulfillment of God's promise to Abraham. In the death and resurrection of Jesus, the promise that through Abraham "all the families of the earth shall be blessed" is fully realized (Gen 12:3). The birth of Isaac, Abraham's promised son, is simply the first step in the redemption initiated by the covenant. The promise is good news not just for Abraham, but for the whole world.

## APPLICATION

The story of Abraham and Sarah's life is not simply about the unfolding of God's promise and faithfulness to the patriarchal couple; it is the story of God revealing himself to those attempting to follow his promise. It is a story of discovering God's character.

When God called Abraham out of Ur, Abraham unquestioningly followed him (Gen 12:1). Yet decades later, when God announced that Sarah would have a son in her old age, both Abraham and Sarah responded with laughter, unable to suppress their doubt (Gen 17:17; 18:12). Abraham and Sarah didn't have the full picture of God's plan, but their laughter also revealed that they did not have a full understanding of the extent of God's power. They had not yet learned that nothing is too difficult for Yahweh (Gen 18:14).

When faced with challenges in our journey of faith, it may become difficult to imagine how God's unlimited ability will pull us through. When we experience loss or pain, we may be unable to place our confidence in God's goodness. In these cases, we can turn to the Bible to see how God's power and grace manifested in the lives of those who followed him. The Bible does not simply describe God's involvement with humankind—it describes who God is. And, like Abraham and Sarah, we can grow in our understanding of God's character as he reveals himself to us in the story of our lives.

# DISCUSSION

## A Closer Look

1. Reflect on a time when you felt God leading you toward something that you felt was impossible. How did you respond?

_____

_____

_____

2. Consider the difference between obedience as a sign that you're following God versus the means by which you fulfill your obligation to God. Which option makes your faith seem more secure?

_____

_____

_____

## Throughout the Bible

1. Paul showed that circumcision is not required for salvation; it was merely an outward sign of God's covenant. Christianity has outward signs of the covenant in baptism and the taking of communion. How do these signs display God's promises?

_____

_____

2. Since circumcision is not required for believers, reflect on what God does require of us. Read Deuteronomy 10:12–22. What does God require when he calls us to circumcise our hearts?

_____

_____

_____

**Beyond the Bible**

1. Can you think of a time in your life when God reassured you regarding his promises? How did this boost your confidence in his ability to carry out his will?

_____

_____

_____

2. Have you ever been in a situation that required you to patiently endure? How long did it last? How did God grow you during that time? How was the situation resolved, and was God's sovereignty evident throughout?

_____

_____

_____

**Application**

1. When have you ever responded in laughter to God's promise in your own life? How has God convinced you of his omnipotence?

_____

_____

_____

2. How does thinking about the Bible as a description of God's character change your view of God's Word? How does thinking of the Bible as a story that tells us who God is affect the way you view your life story?

_____

_____

_____

## CHAPTER 6

# BARGAINING WITH GOD

*Read Genesis 18:16–33; [19:1–38].*

## SETTING THE STAGE

**Theme.** We've all probably questioned God at some point. When we witness human suffering, we may wonder why he allows such experiences to persist. When disasters inflict tragedy and destruction, we may question why he chooses not to intervene. We wonder what, if anything, devastating situations can teach us about God's righteousness. We may even go so far as to question whether God is truly just.

This is exactly what Abraham did in Genesis 18. After hearing that God was planning to destroy Sodom and Gomorrah, he questioned God directly and tried to negotiate pardon for Sodom: Would God still destroy the city if he found 50 righteous people there? What about 45? Would he pardon it for as few as 10? Throughout his bargaining, Abraham wasn't disrespectful. Rather, his questions showed his concern for upholding God's reputation for righteousness and justice. In all his negotiating, Abraham's chief concern was to know, "Will not the Judge of all the earth do right?" (Gen 18:25 NIV). And as a result of Abraham's actions, God showed him a little more of his character: He is indeed just and merciful, but maybe not in the ways we expect.

**Literary Context:** Abraham's bargaining with God in Genesis 18:16–33 fits into the larger section of Genesis 18–19, which begins with three men visiting Abraham and ends with Lot narrowly escaping from the

destruction of Sodom. In some ways, though, the story actually began earlier in Abraham's life, when he and Lot separated (see Gen 13). Lot chose
the fertile Jordan Valley, in which Sodom was located, and Abraham took
Canaan (Gen 13:5–12). Here, we find the first reference to the wickedness
of Sodom (Gen 13:13).

Later, Abraham came to Lot's defense after a group of Mesopotamian
kings sacked Sodom and made off with spoils and captives, including
Lot (Gen 14:11–12). Abraham defeated the Mesopotamian kings, rescued his nephew, and restored Sodom's possessions (Gen 14:13–16).
When the king of Sodom failed to show appreciation for Abraham's intervention, Abraham disassociated himself from the ruler (Gen 14:21–24; see
Chapter 3). In establishing the wickedness of Sodom, the narrative sets
the stage for its later destruction.

**Historical & Cultural Background:** We don't know the precise locations of Sodom and Gomorrah, though they were most likely situated
somewhere around the Dead Sea ("the sea of the salt"; Gen 14:3). The tra-
ditional view is that Sodom and the related "cities of the Plain" (Gen 13:12)
were on the south end of the Dead Sea. Since Lot escaped to a city called
Zoar (Gen 19:22), and there was a city at the southern point of the Dead
Sea bearing that name, this location is possible. However, when Lot and
Abraham first separated, the text says Lot chose "the plain of the Jordan"
(Gen 13:11), which typically refers to the lush Jordan Valley—an area
northeast of the Dead Sea. The place name "the Plain" is also used here
in the destruction of Sodom episode (Gen 19:17, 25, 28–29) and has been
associated with Sodom since Genesis 13:12.

Recent archaeological excavations also support the northern location.[1]
Within this "Plain" area, archaeologists have uncovered several small
"tells" or mounds containing the ruins of ancient cities. Nearby is a much
larger tell thought to be the most prominent of all the cities of the Plain—
Sodom—now known as Tell el-Hammam.

Archaeologists digging at Tell el-Hammam have uncovered a layer of
ash nearly six-and-a-half feet deep in certain places. Within this ash
layer, they've found various artifacts believed to be from the time of
Abraham. They've also found the remains of bodies and artifacts that
have been smashed and burned, but not in a manner typical of warfare

or earthquakes. Archaeologists describe "skeletons covered by architectural debris, limbs twisted out of normal positions, some thrown on their faces with hyperextended joints, and surrounded in the matrix by human bone scatter such as pieces of ribs, the ends of long bones, and skull fragments."[2] The remains may tell the story of Genesis 19—a catastrophe Abraham was trying to prevent.

Ultimately, Abraham's bargaining on behalf of Sodom was not enough to spare the city. God couldn't find at least 10 righteous people (Gen 18:32), and he rained fire and brimstone on both Sodom and Gomorrah (Gen 19:24-25). Yet Abraham's intercession did result in Lot being spared. As Abraham looked down on the ashes of the cities, the story tells us that "God remembered Abraham" and delivered Lot from the destruction (Gen 19:28-29). For several generations, this layer of ash and its remains reminded people of God's deliverance for the righteous and his wrath against the wicked.

## A CLOSER LOOK

This story begins with Abraham accompanying his three visitors as they depart (Gen 18:16). When they reached a place where they could look down on the city of Sodom, God deliberated—either to himself or to the three visitors—about whether he should inform Abraham of his plans to destroy the city (Gen 18:17). As he was considering, God repeated to himself the promise he made to Abraham (Gen 18:18-19).

While previously God articulated the promise several times, this is the only time he voiced the promise without Abraham as his audience (see Gen 12:1-3, 7; 13:14-17; 15:1-21; 17:1-21). God began by reflecting on an aspect of the promise that had been present from the start: that Abraham would become a great and mighty nation that would bless all the nations of the earth (Gen 18:18; see 12:2-3).

God then stated, "I have chosen [Abraham]" (Gen 18:19). With this statement, the theme of divine election—implicit in the narrative thus far—becomes an explicit aspect of Abraham's story and experience as well as that of God's chosen people (see Deut 7:6-8). God's individual election of Abraham would eventually develop into God's collective election of Israel.

In both Abraham's life and the life of the Israel, election entails blessing and protection for the chosen (Deut 4:39; Isa 65:9), as well as an expectation of obedience to the One who elects (Deut 4:40; 7:9–11; Amos 3:2).

> **Quick Bit:** The Hebrew word *tsedeq* (often translated "righteousness") is often used to refer to what is right or fair (see Lev 19:36). When translated as "justice," it carries a legal sense of innocence (see Deut 16:20). In his speeches, for example, Job claimed that his "vindication," or *tsedeq*, was at stake (Job 6:29). Often, *tsedeq* is used to refer to God's "righteous" or "just" judgments (Psa 9:7–8; Jer 11:20). It appears with *mishpat*, or "judgment," in many instances (Psa 33:5; Prov 1:3; Isa 56:1).

God continued by discussing *why* he chose Abraham. In his previous reiterations of the promise, he had revealed only the results of its fulfillment: that Abraham would have many descendants, become a great nation, and be a blessing. Here, he added a reason: God chose Abraham "to do righteousness and justice" (Gen 18:19b). Abraham was to instruct his children and his entire household in God's ways, in righteousness, and in justice. God was about to give Abraham an opportunity to debate these topics, as these very themes would drive Abraham in his intercession for Sodom.

When God told Abraham that he was considering destroying Sodom and Gomorrah because of their sin, Abraham was troubled. He had risked his life to help these cities when he defeated the Mesopotamian kings in Genesis 14 (see Chapter 3). Even so, Abraham's chief concern centered on God's righteousness and justice.

Abraham's first question to God demonstrates his concern for justice: "Will you also sweep away the righteous with the wicked?" (Gen 18:23). Abraham was distressed that in destroying Sodom, God might also destroy any righteous people living there. Such an act would violate God's righteousness and justice since he would be destroying persons undeserving of such punishment.

> **Quick Bit:** The Hebrew word *mishpat* means "justice" or "judgment." It can refer to laws (Psa 119:7) or the carrying out of legal decisions, as in "executing justice" or "bringing someone into judgment" (Psa 146:7; Eccl 12:14). Proverbs claims that evil men cannot understand *mishpat*—only those who seek God can (Prov 28:5).

God's *mishpat* includes both condemning the guilty and vindicating the righteous (1 Kgs 8:32).

Abraham used strong language to voice his disapproval, twice repeating, "Far be it from you …" (Gen 18:25). This phrase is a strong way of expressing disapproval, equivalent to saying "certainly not." David later used this phrase to emphasize that he refused to harm Saul, God's anointed one (1 Sam 26:11).[3] Abraham's use of the phrase expresses how unthinkable it seemed to him that God, the just Judge of the earth, would destroy the innocent along with the guilty. He began by asking God to spare the city if there were 50 righteous people in it (Gen 18:24).

After God agreed to this request (Gen 18:26), Abraham started to bargain for lower numbers. He did so with respect and humility, recognizing his position before God ("I am dust and ashes"; Gen 18:27) and being careful not to overstep his place ("Please, let not my Lord be angry"; Gen 18:30, 32). Each time he spoke, Abraham asked that God spare the city for the sake of fewer righteous people. With each lower number, Abraham demonstrated greater faith in God's mercy as he asked God to spare an entire city of wicked people for the sake of only a few righteous.

We don't know why the negotiation ended at 10 righteous people (Gen 18:32). It is possible that the number 10 represented totality for the author of the story.[4] Regardless of the reason, Abraham had made his point by the time the bargaining ended. He had appealed to God's mercy, and God had agreed to spare the entire city for the sake of 10 righteous people.

It is important to note that Abraham didn't try to convince God to change his plans. As one scholar says, "Abraham was not trying to talk God into doing something against his will, for he was convinced of the righteousness of God."[5] God's justice would prohibit him from punishing the innocent, and his mercy would allow him to save the wicked from punishment. Abraham, who was chosen "to do righteousness and justice" and to instruct his descendants to do the same (Gen 18:19), showed a clear understanding of these facets of God's character.

Ultimately, Sodom lacked even 10 righteous people, and God destroyed both Sodom and Gomorrah by raining down fire and brimstone (Gen 19:24–25).

Even so, Abraham's intercession was not futile. God showed his mercy in a way that exceeded Abraham's negotiation.

After the cities' destruction, Abraham returned to the place where he had negotiated with God and looked down on the ashes where the cities once stood. At this point, the narrative explains that when God destroyed the cities, he "remembered Abraham" and delivered Lot (Gen 19:29). The term *zakhar*, meaning "to remember," is often used in the context of God remembering and staying loyal to his covenant (Exod 2:24; Psa 105:8). Here, it speaks to the privileged position Abraham held ("I have chosen him"; Gen 18:19) and indicates that God demonstrated mercy in the midst of judgment.

## THROUGHOUT THE BIBLE

Abraham was not the only character to question God directly regarding matters of righteousness and justice. When the people of Israel worshiped the golden calf, Moses interceded on their behalf and asked God to spare them from destruction (Exod 32:11–12). He asked God to "remember" (*zakhar*) his promises to Abraham, Isaac, and Jacob (Exod 32:13). In this instance, God listened to Moses and relented from destroying the people (Exod 32:14).

Perhaps the most famous example of someone openly questioning God is Job. Likely a contemporary of Abraham, Job was described by God as the most blameless and upright person on earth (Job 1:8; 2:2). God allowed Satan to afflict Job, destroying his wealth, family, and causing him to break out in sores. In a series of speeches, Job defended himself against his three friends and accused God of treating him unfairly.

Job addressed God forcefully and bluntly. He demanded to know why God had afflicted him (Job 7:20–21; 10:2–3), and he accused God of acting unjustly (Job 9:22–24). Throughout his speeches, Job asserted his own innocence (Job 6:10; 9:15, 20–21), but his main concern was understanding why God had allowed him to suffer so much when he had done nothing to deserve such punishment (Job 13:22–23). Job argued with his friends that injustice does occur: The wicked are not always punished, and the innocent are not always rewarded (Job 21:7–19). He questioned why God does not "set times for judgment" and allows the wicked to prosper (Job 24:1 NIV; see Job 24:1–12). He expressed distress at what felt to him like unjust treatment from God (Job 27:2).

While Abraham's petitions showed humility and respect, some of Job's speeches seem shockingly bold. And although Job repented after God responded (Job 42:2–6),[6] God actually commended him for speaking "what is right" (Job 42:7). Despite Job's strong questions and challenges, God did not charge him with wrongdoing because Job conveyed his situation accurately. Not only was he innocent, he was suffering *because* he was innocent—he was the most blameless man on earth (Job 1:8). Job, like Abraham, questioned God, and his questions came from a proper understanding of God's righteousness and justice.

The lament psalms also portray people questioning God's righteousness and justice. These laments show psalmists complaining about their suffering and asking God for help. The psalmists often appealed to their own honor as they asked God to hear them (Pss 4:1; 27:7; 55:1–2; 143:7).

For example, in Psalm 7, the psalmist asserts his innocence before God, saying that if he has done wrong, then God should punish him (Psa 7:3–5). Like Abraham, the psalmist describes God as "a righteous judge" and, confident in his own integrity, he asks God to judge him (Psa 7:8–11). Similarly, the psalmist of Psalm 17 asks God to vindicate him because he is innocent (Psa 17:2–5).

In these examples, the psalmists, like Job, believed that God is righteous and just. Because they were innocent, they considered their suffering to be unjust. God, the righteous Judge, should deliver them from their trouble.

These ancient passages hold many lessons for us today. Like Abraham, Job, and the psalmists, we should not be afraid to be honest with God about how we feel. God is not afraid of our questions, and he hears us even when we feel that he has rejected us. Even so, we may not get the response we desire. God destroyed Sodom, and he never told Job the reason for his suffering. Yet God remembered Abraham and showed his mercy in a way Abraham did not expect. Job was given a powerful reminder of God's sovereignty and eventually experienced God's generous mercy, as God restored his family, health, and fortune (Job 42:10–17).

## BEYOND THE BIBLE

Questioning God isn't a phenomenon unique to the Bible. Even before Abraham's encounter in Genesis 18:22–33, people wrestled to understand apparent contradictions in divine behavior. People have always thought that God (or "the gods," in the eyes of Israel's pagan neighbors) adheres to some standard of justice. Yet whenever people perceive injustice, they tend to reconsider their assumptions.

> **Quick Bit:** Akkad was a city in ancient Mesopotamia that flourished around 2500 BC. Likely founded by Nimrod as Accad (see Gen 10:10), it rose to prominence during the reign of King Sargon (ca. 2334–2279 BC). It was destroyed around 2150 BC and was never rebuilt.

This struggle can be seen in a poem dating to roughly the same period as Abraham. In *I Will Praise the Lord of Wisdom* (also known as *The Poem of the Righteous Sufferer*), a pious worshiper from the ancient city of Akkad struggled to understand the actions of his god. Despite acting correctly, this worshiper experienced suffering. Similar to Job, he voiced his inability to understand why.[7] He wrote:

> I wish I knew that these things would be pleasing to one's god!
> What is good for oneself may be offense to one's god,
> What in one's own heart seems despicable may be proper to
>     one's god.
> Who can know the will of the gods in heaven?
> Who can understand the plans of the underworld gods?
> Where have humans learned the way of a god?
> He who was alive yesterday is dead today.
> One moment he is worried, the next he is boisterous.
> One moment he is singing a joyful song,
> A moment later he wails like a professional mourner.[8]

When the behavior of this Akkadian god seemed contradictory, this worshiper asked questions, just as Abraham did. Considered alongside the stories of Abraham and Job, this poem shows that asking questions is a very human and universal response to suffering and destruction. Abraham was not unique in this regard—his story is not an exception.

Yet Abraham bargained with God on the basis of his character. The patriarch knew of God's righteousness and justice. He framed his proposal that God spare the city for the sake of a righteous remnant by highlighting the inconsistency between Sodom's impending doom and his nature. God allowed Abraham the freedom to voice his concern, but he ultimately took just action by destroying the wicked city.

# APPLICATION

We don't often approach God the way Abraham did in Genesis 18:16–33. We tend to be leery of questioning or negotiating with him. It seems disrespectful or even sacrilegious to question God or voice our discontent. However, the Bible contains many examples of people who did just that— and they did so in a respectful manner.

Sometimes we try to bargain with God. We promise certain behaviors or actions if God will grant our requests. This type of bargaining shows a faulty understanding of what God desires. When Abraham negotiated with God, he did not do so based on what he could bring. He did not say, "God, if you spare Sodom, I'll offer extra sacrifices." Instead, Abraham negotiated based on God's character, appealing to his justice and righteousness. In doing so, Abraham showed that he understood what is important to God.

Other righteous people in the Bible also focused on God's character when they approached God. When Moses asked God to refrain from punishing Israel for the golden calf incident, he appealed specifically to God's reputation and his faithfulness, asking God how it would look to the Egyptians if he destroyed his own people (Exod 32:12). The psalmists wrestled with suffering and pain and presented their complaints to God, yet always with a focus on his character. Even Job's complaints were based on a view of God's attributes; Job could not reconcile his understanding of God's righteousness with the severe suffering he was experiencing.

In the Sermon on the Mount, Jesus encouraged his followers to approach God in prayer. God is not afraid of our questions; he wants to talk with us and hear our struggles. We can tell him exactly what we are going through and trust that he understands our concerns and weaknesses. Yet Jesus also instructed his followers to put God first—to "seek first the kingdom of God and his righteousness" (Matt 6:33 ESV). God may not respond in the way we expect or want him to, and we will not always understand how his mercy and grace is working to faithfully complete his work in our lives (1 Cor 13:12; Phil 1:6). However, we can be confident that the Judge of all the earth will do right.

# DISCUSSION

## A Closer Look

1. God chose Abraham "to do righteousness and justice" and to teach his descendants to keep the way of God. In what ways does your life reflect these aspects of God's character? How can you better demonstrate God's righteousness and justice to others?

_____

_____

_____

2. Think of tragedies or injustices you have seen or experienced. Did they cause you to doubt the justice of God? Have you ever experienced a situation, like Abraham, where you questioned God? What have these experiences taught you about his nature?

_____

_____

## Throughout the Bible

1. What can we learn from the way Abraham and Job questioned God? How does their understanding of God's righteousness and justice affect how they view punishment and suffering? What can we learn from God's response to Job in Job 38:1–41:34?

_____

_____

2. In Psalms 7 and 17, the psalmist asks God to judge him and vindicate him. Have you ever felt like you needed to be vindicated? How did you express yourself to God?

_____

_____

## Beyond the Bible

1. Have you ever questioned God's actions? Have you ever appealed to his justice at times you saw injustice all around you? How does Abraham's plea help you see and understand God's sovereignty more clearly?

_____

_____

_____

2. Do you feel the freedom to question God in difficult times? Does the Bible allow for this? What passages might speak against such action? How can you appropriately give voice to your sense of perceived injustice, particularly during difficult times?

_____

_____

_____

## Application

1. How can a fuller understanding of the character of God enhance your prayer life? Does thinking about who God is change the way you pray? In what ways?

_____

_____

_____

2. Do you know anyone—in your church or in your family—who demonstrates these facets of God's character? Have you ever known them to question God? What could you learn from their experience?

_____

_____

_____

## CHAPTER 7

# GOD'S FAITHFULNESS DESPITE RELAPSE

*Read Genesis 20:1–18; 21:22–34.*

## SETTING THE STAGE

**Theme.** One of the most frustrating aspects of the Christian life is our continual struggle with sin—especially our tendency to repeat sins for which we've already been forgiven. Even though we know the right thing to do, we often fall into old habits when we face difficult circumstances. Often these habits reflect our lack of trust in God and his promises.

The great women and men of the Bible shared this struggle in their attempt to follow God. In Genesis 12:10–20, Abraham doubted the promises he had just received from God (blessing, children, land; see Gen 12:2–3, 7). He fled to Egypt at the first sign of trouble (see Chapter 2). While there, he jeopardized God's promises by lying to Pharaoh's officials about Sarah's identity. When we read Genesis 20, the story feels all too familiar: Abraham repeated this same sin—using the same lie—and failed to trust in God's promises and protection while in foreign territory. Instead of exhibiting faith, he fell back on his old lie that Sarah was his sister in an attempt to avoid death. And yet God mercifully used Abraham's repeated sin to reaffirm his covenant *faithfulness*—despite his servant's *faithlessness*.

**Literary Context.** Although Abraham is remembered as a man of faith, he still encountered setbacks. Genesis 20 begins with a familiar phrase:

"And Abraham said about Sarah his wife, 'She is my sister' " (Gen 20:2). When we read this statement, we recall the last time Abraham used this lie and its aftermath (see Gen 12:13, 15). We remember that things didn't go well in that situation, and we begin to expect similar results here. We also recall that since God intervened then, turning evil into good, he will probably act similarly here—a pattern that has come to typify Abraham's life.

At first glance, it may seem surprising that Abraham lapsed into this old sin. But 25 years had passed since God first promised him an heir, and he was getting older. As the end of Abraham's life approached, he was becoming desperate. Earlier, he and Sarah had tried to bring about the promise on their own (see Gen 16:1–4), perhaps thinking that God needed *their* help. But God was very specific in his promise: A son would be born to Abraham *by* Sarah (see Gen 17:19). Abraham's goal at this point was to stay alive, so as he approached Gerar, he reverted to a plan that would ensure his survival, even though it jeopardized God's promise.

As often happens in our own spiritual journeys, Abraham failed to learn from his mistakes. The lesson he was supposed to learn in Genesis 12 failed to take root, so in Genesis 20, he regressed to his previous sin. Even so, the big picture of Abraham's life testifies that God provides for and protects his people, despite their moral failures.

**Historical & Cultural Background.** The stories of God's faithfulness to Abraham are told within the context of Abraham's sojourning. In the ancient Near East, the word "sojourning" described the activity of a traveler in a foreign place. Sojourners entered a land in which they had no familial connection, and they either took up residence or spent a lengthy period of time there. This concept is used to describe the lives of the patriarchs in Genesis and is important for understanding their travels and journeys with God (see Gen 12:10; 20:1; 21:34; 26:3; 32:4; Exod 6:4).

> **Quick Bit:** The Hebrew word *gur* (meaning "sojourner") refers to someone who travels through or establishes residence in a foreign land. This verb brackets the Abraham and Abimelech stories, occurring in Genesis 20:1 and Genesis 21:34 (as well as Gen 21:23). Within Abraham's story, this word describes his spiritual journey as well as his physical journey from Ur to the promised land. Abraham moved all he had—his family, livestock, and possessions—in obedience to God's call.

Abraham's sojourning became synonymous with a life of faith. What is surprising about the events of Genesis 20—which occurred later in his life—is that he repeated a mistake he made at the beginning of his journey. This relapse reveals that Abraham still had fear and doubt concerning God's promises. Yet these very human qualities are what make him so easy for us to relate to.

Our Christian life is often compared to a journey or a walk (see Gen 5:22, 24; 6:9; 17:1; 2 Cor 5:7; 1 John 1:7). This metaphor communicates both the length and nature of our spiritual expedition: It is a long, slow process. Along the way, we encounter various trials that test our commitment to God. These trials can dissuade us, as they dissuaded Abraham, from living according to the promises of God. Often, our greatest victories occur as we overcome these temptations, while our most dismal failures occur when we give in to them.

The metaphor of a walk or journey developed from the lives of the patriarchs, particularly from Abraham. It refers not only to his actual movement from place to place, but also to his journey with God. His life is retold around his "walk"—his life of sojourning where God led him and, at times, where he did not. When Abraham lived confidently in full assurance of God's promises, things went well for him. When he attempted to supplement those promises or work toward them in his own creativity and timing, things went poorly. These truths are as real for us today as they were for Abraham thousands of years ago.

## A CLOSER LOOK

Genesis 20 begins by noting Abraham's southern sojourn. At some point, he made a trip northward to the city of Gerar, perhaps to trade or feed his flocks (see 1 Chr 4:39–40; 2 Chr 14:13).[1] It is at that point that we encounter Abraham's old lie (Gen 20:2; compare 12:13).

News of Abraham's arrival had made its way back to Abimelech, the king of Gerar. At this time, although Abraham was an elderly, nomadic herdsman, he was also very wealthy; he owned large amounts of livestock and led his own private army (see Gen 14:14). It would have been politically advantageous for Abimelech to take a member of Abraham's household into his harem; marrying one of Abraham's close relatives would ensure that Abraham would never go to war against him. Since Abraham was old and had no children by Sarah, his lie ("she is my sister") was believable.

After Abimelech took Sarah into his harem, God intervened to ensure that his promise—that Sarah would have a son—would be fulfilled (see Gen 18:10). God appeared to Abimelech and indicted him (Gen 20:3). The king responded by appealing to God's justice: Since he had not yet consummated the marriage—a point the text makes clear (Gen 20:4; "approached" is a euphemism for sexual intercourse)—he considered himself innocent. Yet the king also recognized the legitimacy of God's indictment and the gravity of the accusation. Adultery wasn't merely a Jewish prohibition; other ancient Near Eastern law codes viewed it as a punishable offense as well.[2]

Since he did not know Abraham's God—Yahweh—Abimelech addressed him as "Lord" (*adonai* in Hebrew), a deferential, respectful title. He asked, "Will you even kill a righteous people?" (Gen 20:4). Not only does this mirror the question Abraham asked of God regarding the destruction of Sodom (see Gen 18:23, 25), but a form of the word *tsaddiq* ("righteous") is also used to describe Abraham (the offending party here) in Genesis 15:6. In addition, Abimelech appealed to his own integrity (*tham* in Hebrew) in Genesis 20:5, using the same word God used when commanding Abraham to "walk before me and be blameless" (Gen 17:1). The contrast between the two men is intentional: In every respect, the foreign king acted in the way Abraham *should* have acted.

God acknowledged Abimelech's integrity (Gen 20:6) but put it to the test: Since he was aware of the grievance, he needed to make it right; failure to do so would result in his death. God also asserted that he prevented Abimelech from committing this great sin (consummating the marriage and committing adultery). The text leaves us wondering exactly how this was accomplished. The end of this chapter tells us that God caused the women in Abimelech's harem to be barren, but this would hardly have prevented the king from consummating the marriage; he wouldn't know about their barrenness until sometime after the fact. It is possible that God caused the king (and perhaps the men of his household) to be temporarily impotent. Perhaps this is what he needed to be "healed" or cured of in Genesis 20:17. But the story's main point is that God intervened to protect his promise of a son. The birth of Isaac, which follows immediately in Genesis 21:1–7, was not the result of a sexual union between Abimelech and Sarah.

Obediently, the king awoke early and took action (Gen 20:8). Before summoning Abraham, he first called his court officials to tell them about his encounter with God. After being interrogated by the king, Abraham attempted to justify his deceit by saying, "Because I thought, surely there is no fear of God in this place" (Gen 20:11). Yet the story tells us that earlier, when Abimelech's officials heard the words of God, "[they] were very afraid" (see Gen 20:8). Abraham feared man rather than God and repeated his previous sin, whereas the men who did not know God feared him. Abimelech and his men obeyed unquestioningly after their first encounter with God, and they did so at the earliest possible opportunity.

> **Quick Bit:** In Genesis 20, the Hebrew verb *yr'* (and its derivatives) describes reverence, respect, or awe for God and his power—not simply fear. In Genesis 20:8, when Abimelech recounted his interaction with God the night before, he and his court officials responded with reverence and awe. Ironically, Abraham lied because he thought that the men of Gerar didn't fear God (Gen 20:2, 11).

After previously declaring Abraham righteous (see Gen 15:6), God then used this righteous foreign king to rebuke him. Abimelech questioned Abraham about the motivation behind his deception (Gen 20:9–10). He showed himself to be morally superior to Abraham by appealing to a seemingly universal value system—"You have done things to me that should not be done"—that Abraham ignored (Gen 20:10).[3] Compared to Abimelech's defense in Genesis 20:4–5, Abraham's excuse was weak and unconvincing. Whereas Abimelech offended Abraham unintentionally, Abraham acted deliberately, motivated by self-preservation. He thought that Abimelech would choose to kill him rather than commit adultery, and he considered Gerar to be without fear of God or respect for human life.

> **Quick Bit:** Since Abraham was a sojourner, he was not legally protected in the same manner as the citizens of Gerar. He was vulnerable

to the same sort of mistreatment that the visitors to Sodom experienced in the previous episode (see Gen 19:5, 9). These recent events, and Abraham's need to be alive in order to obtain God's promise, likely contributed to his relapse into an old sin.

Abraham further attempted to justify his lie by explaining that Sarah was his half-sister (Gen 20:12). Such a relationship was later banned by the law of Moses (see Lev 20:17; Deut 27:22), but at this point (pre-law) it was still socially acceptable to marry half-siblings. Even so, Abraham could not hide that his original motivation for explaining this relationship was to deceive Abimelech.

The king, who still needed Abraham to pray for him (see Gen 20:7), probably recognized that Abraham's defense lacked substance. Yet he chose not to reply. Instead, Abimelech restored Sarah to Abraham, publically exonerated her, gave them both lavish gifts, and invited them to continue sojourning wherever they pleased in Gerar (Gen 20:14–16). Abraham subsequently prayed for Abimelech, and God healed the king and his household (Gen 20:17).

The story ends by recalling God's divine intervention (Gen 20:18). Abimelech presented a threat to the fulfillment of God's promise to give Abraham and Sarah a son. Since God was about to fulfill this promise (see Gen 21:1–7), he had to intercede. If left to Abraham and Sarah—who repeatedly jeopardized God's plan—the promise might not have been fulfilled; it was realized only by the grace of God.

Abraham's encounters with Abimelech did not end here; the two meet again in the following chapter (see Gen 21:22–34). In light of the events of Genesis 20, this episode opens with the two men making a covenant to deal truthfully and loyally with one another (Gen 21:22–24). Sometime after this, as Abraham sojourned under Abimelech's jurisdiction, a dispute arose over a well. Abimelech's servants had seized the well from Abraham's servants, apparently apart from the king's knowledge (see Gen 21:25–26). Abimelech's encounter with Abraham's God in the previous chapter, as well as his knowledge that Abraham was God's prophet (see Gen 20:7), predisposed him to act favorably toward Abraham (see Gen 21:27–34). As the story concludes, God's demonstrates his faithfulness, despite Abraham's repeated sin in Genesis 20.

# THROUGHOUT THE BIBLE

Later biblical writers chose to overlook Abraham's shortcomings. Although the text describes a man who wrestled with fear, doubt, dishonesty, and repeated sin—struggles that are common in our human experience—subsequent generations remember him for his remarkable faith. What's more, he is remembered as "God's friend" (see Jas 2:23)—one who shared a close relationship with him and whom God always protected.

> **Quick Bit:** In Genesis 20:7, God refers to Abraham as a prophet. The term is translated from the Hebrew word *navi* and generally refers to one who speaks on behalf of God—one who communicates God's word. Occasionally, *navi* takes on an alternative meaning, depending on the context. Here, it is used to describe Abraham's role as an intercessor—one who prays to God on behalf of someone else. The word is used similarly elsewhere in the OT (see Num 14:13–19; 1 Sam 7:8; 12:19, 23).

As mentioned in Chapter 2, Psalm 105 alludes to various aspects of the patriarchs' sojourning and has many parallels with the Abraham and Abimelech story. While extolling God's providential care for the Israelites (even in light of their repeated mistakes), the psalmist recalls God's promises to Abraham and his offspring (Psa 105:8–11). In Psalm 105:12, he recounts their sojourning, bringing to mind Genesis 20:1, 15; 21:34. Psalm 105:14 evokes the imagery of God rebuking Abimelech in Genesis 20:3, 6–7. Furthermore, the psalmist, when speaking on behalf of God, refers to the patriarchs as "prophets" (Psa 105:15; *navi* in Hebrew)—the same word used of Abraham in Genesis 20:7 (the only time a patriarch is called "prophet" in the Pentateuch).

The psalmist's purpose in doing all of this is clear: Remembering God's covenant faithfulness to Abraham (through his repeated mistakes) will help readers worship in a more informed way (see Psa 105:1–6). God's faithfulness to Abraham in the Abimelech episode is characteristic of his dealings with the nation of Israel as a whole. By remembering God's wondrous protection and faithfulness to Abraham and his family, the psalmist recalls God's same activity in the life of the nation. This is even more amazing in light of Israel's history of covenant unfaithfulness. The only appropriate response for the people is to worship God.

The same concept is true for us today. As we read Abraham stories, we're reminded of our own shortcomings in light of God's promises. We often fail to believe them fully—particularly when times get tough—and we revert to sinful behavior. But when we see God's continued faithfulness through our mistakes, our response should be one of gratitude and worship.

## BEYOND THE BIBLE

As noted in Chapter 2, it seems strange that Abraham feared the Egyptians would kill him for Sarah, who was 60 years old at the time. The *Genesis Apocryphon* imaginatively filled in the gaps for us. We can raise a similar question here: Why would Abimelech want to marry a 90-year-old woman (compare Gen 17:17; 21:5)?

> **Quick Bit:** The Babylonian Talmud is a rabbinic commentary on the Jewish law written between AD 500 and 600. The Hebrew word *talmud* means "instruction" or "learning."

In Genesis 12, the first occurrence of the wife–sister lie, the biblical text explicitly mentions Sarah's beauty as the reason for Pharaoh's desire. But no mention is made in chapter 20 about Sarah's beauty. This led rabbis in the first few centuries AD to suggest something miraculous had occurred. In the Babylonian Talmud, a collection of Jewish traditions, Rabbi Hisda proposed, "After the flesh got worn and the skin wrinkled, the flesh became pleasurable, the wrinkles were smoothed out, and beauty was restored" (see b. B. Mes. 87A).[4] This would account for Abimelech's interest in Sarah, but the Bible says nothing of the sort. Like the *Genesis Apocryphon* (see Chapter 2), this excerpt from the Babylonian Talmud shows how ancient interpreters sought to understand difficult passages in the OT.

However, such an approach makes a difficult passage unnecessarily complicated. A more likely solution can be found by considering this episode in its ancient Near Eastern context. In the time of Abraham, marriages often served as alliances—a concept seen throughout the OT (see 1 Kgs 3:1). Abimelech knew of Abraham's great wealth and power and wanted him as an ally. He knew Abraham had defeated four kings with an army of 318 men (see Gen 14:14-15). By marrying into the family, he could ensure that the Abraham would not go to war with him.

Abraham's repeated sin—and the questions associated with it—draw our attention to a larger issue. They emphasize God's role in the story of his people. Sarah's son had to come from both Abraham *and* Sarah to fulfill God's promise (see Gen 17:18-19; 18:10, 14). Consequently, God prevented the people of Gerar from procreating so that Sarah could not be impregnated by Abimelech. Immediately following this episode, God fulfilled his word with the birth of Isaac (although roughly a year transpired). It is God who promises, provides, and protects, and God is faithful to his promises, despite the repeated sins of his people.

## APPLICATION

In times of difficulty or uncertainty, it's easy to relapse into familiar habits—even if we're aware that what we're doing is wrong. When Abraham once again found himself feeling threatened in an unfamiliar land, he fell back into an old sin characterized by fear, doubt, and dishonesty. Yet God brought Abraham through the mess he got himself into, despite his weakness, and he brought about the promise of an heir according to his word. Even when we fall short in our struggle against sin, God remains faithful to his promises.

Our struggle against sin can seem never ending, despite forgiveness and faith in Christ. In Romans 7:14-25, the Apostle Paul voices this frustration, remarking, "I do not understand my own actions. For I do not do what I want, but I do the very thing I hate" (Rom 7:15 NRSV). Yet Paul also knows that our salvation, which is secured in Christ and with the indwelling Holy Spirit, gives us the power to overcome sin and trust God's promises in every situation. Because of this, Paul could exclaim, "Wretched man that I am! Who will rescue me from this body of death? *Thanks be to God through Jesus Christ our Lord!*" (Rom 7:24-25a).

When we face times of uncertainty, we can also take comfort knowing that God is in control. As he demonstrates in Abraham's story, all life—and the ability to create and sustain it—is in his hands. If God even takes care of the birds and the grass (Matt 6:25-34), we, his children, can have confidence that he will take care of us in every situation (John 1:12; Rom 8:14; Gal 3:26). As Jesus said, "For your heavenly Father knows that you need all these things. But seek first his kingdom and righteousness, and all these things will be added to you" (Matt 6:32b–33).

When faced with the challenge of relapsing into old sins, we need to remember that Jesus' death secured the means to overcome this struggle. Because of Christ's sacrifice and the assistance of the Holy Spirit, we can trust in God's promises in the face of all opposition and uncertainty.

# DISCUSSION

## A Closer Look

1. Recall a time in your life when God's faithfulness contrasted your faith-lessness. What did your experience of God's continued faithfulness teach you about his character? How did it inspire you to be more confident in your faith?

_____

_____

_____

2. How does Abraham's sojourning serve as a means of understanding your own walk of faith?

_____

_____

_____

## Throughout the Bible

1. How do you think God views your shortcomings? How does the death and resurrection of Christ affect God's view of us?

_____

_____

_____

2. If a chapter in the Psalms were written about God's providential care and protection in your life, what kinds of things would it include? How would you worship God differently because of them?

_____

_____

_____

## Beyond the Bible

1. How do you find solutions when you run across difficult passages in the Bible? How might an understanding of culture and context help to inform your decisions about such passages?

_____

_____

_____

2. Can you think of an alliance you've made that didn't turn out as you had hoped? Can you see evidence of God's grace in that situation? In what ways has God protected you from poor decision-making?

_____

_____

_____

## Application

1. In what ways is the realization of God's control over life a comfort to you? How does this help you to more fully trust in him?

_____

_____

_____

2. In light of the story of Abraham and Abimelech, what steps can you take in your life to keep from repeating old sins?

_____

_____

_____

## CHAPTER 8

# OF SONS AND SACRIFICE

*Read Genesis 21:1–21; 22:1–24.*

## SETTING THE STAGE

**Theme.** We have all experienced tests of our faith—situations that require us to trust that God will provide. In these times, the question becomes: How do we respond? Do we allow fear and doubt to control us, or do we trust God with an extreme faith?

Abraham experienced many tests of faith in his life. At times, he responded obediently and trusted in God's promises. Other times, however, he responded out of fear or tried to take matters into his own hands. In Genesis 22, Abraham received one final extreme test of his faith—a test that came directly from God (Gen 22:1).

**Literary Context.** After years of uncertainty, the promised birth finally happened. Sarah welcomed a son, whom Abraham named Isaac (Gen 21:2–3). Abraham circumcised him when he was eight days old, just as God had commanded (Gen 21:4; see 17:12). The pieces of the promise finally fell into place: Abraham had the promised son through Sarah, just as God said. Emphasizing Sarah's inability to bear children (Gen 17:17; 18:11–12) and Abraham's old age, the Bible testifies that God truly worked a miracle.

The various mentions of Abraham's age anchor the progression of events in real time and show the accuracy of God's promise. When Abraham was 99 years old (Gen 17:1, 24), God twice stated that he would give Abraham and Sarah a son within the year (Gen 17:21; 18:14). Sarah had Isaac when Abraham was 100 years old (Gen 21:5), showing that God was true to his word.

The mentions of Abraham's age also indicate how long he had to wait for God to fulfill his promise. Abraham was 75 years old when God first called him to leave Ur (Gen 12:4), 86 years old when Ishmael was born (Gen 16:16), and 100 years old when Isaac was finally born (Gen 21:5). Abraham waited 25 years for God to take the first step in fulfilling his promise to make him "a great nation" (Gen 12:2). During this period, Abraham faced many situations that tested his faith. Now, after God's promise to provide an heir had finally been fulfilled, Abraham would face his greatest test of faith yet.

**Historical & Cultural Background.** In Genesis 22, God instructed Abraham to take Isaac up to a mountain and offer him as a burnt offering. A common type of sacrifice in the ancient Near East, burnt offerings required that the sacrificial animal be entirely burnt on the altar, possibly as a sign of total devotion to the deity. Offering a sacrifice closely connected to the individual's desire to obtain blessing or favor from the gods.[1] Sacrifices typically involved sheep, birds, or bulls. Human sacrifice was probably rare in the ancient Near East, but the fact that the Mosaic law specifically prohibited it suggests that it was sometimes practiced (Lev 18:21; Deut 12:13).

Burnt offerings in the OT were made for various reasons, including for thanksgiving and as atonement for guilt. After the flood, Noah offered burnt offerings of clean animals and birds on an altar (Gen 8:20). After God brought Israel out of Egypt, Jethro (Moses' father-in-law) offered a burnt offering in thanksgiving (Exod 18:8–12). Job offered burnt offerings on behalf of his children in case they sinned (Job 1:5). He also offered burnt offerings to atone for his friends' error in not speaking correctly about God (Job 42:7–9).[2]

We are not told how Abraham felt when he heard God's instruction to sacrifice his only son; there is no record of what was going through his mind.[3] Abraham had recently sent away his first son, Ishmael, with Hagar (Gen 21:10–14), so losing his other son, Isaac, would have been devastating. However, Abraham showed extreme faith in God's promise. God had recently reassured him that Isaac *would* be the heir to the promise

(Gen 21:12). Here, Abraham showed such strong trust in God's promise that he was willing to sacrifice Isaac, his only heir.

In some ways, this story is the climax of Abraham's faith. Aside from the account of Sarah's death (Gen 23:1–20) and a listing of his other descendants (Gen 25:1–6), this is the final account in which Abraham is the central figure. Despite his past failures, Abraham's story ends with a demonstration of extreme faith that serves as an example for our own efforts to be faithful to God.

# A CLOSER LOOK

Genesis 21 opens by recounting the birth of Isaac (Gen 21:1–7)—the high point of Abraham's life and the culmination of several years of waiting. Yet, the account of Isaac's birth is unexpectedly subdued. The simplicity with which this event is narrated contrasts with our expectations as readers. Shouldn't this seminal event receive more attention and fanfare? After 25 years, the promise was finally fulfilled, and yet the details are presented matter-of-factly.

In emphasizing that God did "as he had promised" (Gen 21:1) and that the event happened "at the appointed time that God had told him" (Gen 21:2), the text focuses on God's part in keeping his promise. Abraham and Sarah's reactions are muted and overshadowed by the sequence of events: Sarah conceived, the boy was born, Abraham called him Isaac, and Abraham circumcised Isaac. The only dialogue is Sarah expressing delight over the fulfillment of what she had thought was impossible (Gen 21:6–7).

> **Quick Bit:** Sarah's reaction to Isaac's birth plays on the meaning of his name in Hebrew. Isaac, or *yitschaq*, means "he laughed." When Sarah said that "God has made laughter (*tsechoq*) for me," there is a sense of irony: God's earlier reiteration of the promise had provoked both Abraham and Sarah to laugh in surprise and disbelief. Genesis 17:17 says "Abraham ... laughed (*yitschaq*)," whereas Genesis 18:12 says "Sarah laughed (*titschaq*)." The promise both laughed at and regarded as impossible had come to pass. Now they laughed in joy instead of doubt. Isaac's name was a daily reminder for them of God's power over the impossible.

If this were merely a story about God fulfilling his promise, it could end here with Abraham and Sarah finally receiving the son and heir they had always hoped for. But the story of Abraham is also about his faith: the faith that drove him to leave his country at God's command (Gen 12:4), the faith that led him to take up arms against mighty kings who kidnapped his kin (Gen 14:14-15), the faith that enabled him to circumcise every male in his household (Gen 17:23-27), and the faith that empowered him to bargain with God over the fate of the righteous in a wicked city (Gen 18:22-33). Abraham's resolve had been tested repeatedly, and now it would be tested again—especially when it came to his relationships with his two sons.

Isaac may have been the promised son, but Ishmael was still the eldest. As the firstborn, Ishmael was technically Abraham's legal heir. If Hagar had remained merely a "slave woman" (as Sarah called her in Gen 21:10), then Ishmael would not have had this blessing available to him. However, Sarah had given Hagar to Abraham as a wife (Gen 16:4)—a status necessary for her to serve as a surrogate mother and provide Abraham with an heir. Now, with Isaac as the true son of the promise, the implications of Sarah's scheme from years before came full circle—and it wasn't long before she realized it.

The narrative covers the first few years of Isaac's life in a single sentence: "And the child grew and was weaned" (Gen 21:8). The occasion of his weaning was the backdrop for Sarah's demand that Abraham send Ishmael away. While the family was having a party to celebrate Isaac's weaning (Gen 21:8), Sarah saw Ishmael "laughing" (*metsacheq*, the same basic word as Isaac's name, *yitschaq*). The text does not specifically tell us what Sarah saw Ishmael do, but her strong reaction—telling Abraham to throw Hagar and Ishmael out of the household—is often read as an indication that Ishmael was mocking, taunting, or abusing Isaac.

The reality is likely far less insidious; Ishmael was probably only "playing," another possible meaning of *metsacheq*. The text simply says he was "laughing" or "playing" without indicating with whom. Whatever happened, Sarah used this as an opportunity to have Ishmael—the obstacle to Isaac's full inheritance—removed from the family. Her assertion in Genesis 21:10 makes clear that this was her motivation: "Drive out this slave woman and her son, for the son of this slave woman will not be heir with my son, with Isaac." Here, Sarah could not bring herself to refer to either Ishmael or Hagar by name. Rather, she emphasized Hagar's former status as a slave and identified Ishmael as merely the "son of this slave woman," refusing to acknowledge that he was also Abraham's son.

Yet Abraham was troubled by Sarah's request and her attitude toward "his son" (Gen 21:11). What followed was a test of Abraham's faith regarding his relationship with Ishmael—his firstborn son. Without condoning Sarah's request, God told Abraham to "listen to everything that Sarah said to you" and assured him that Ishmael's future had been accounted for in his plan: Ishmael, too, would be made into a "nation, for he is your offspring" (Gen 21:13).

Still, disinheriting Ishmael could not have been easy for Abraham. As readers, we already know the big picture: Isaac was the promised heir. The story keeps our focus on Isaac by moving quickly through this sequence of events: Sarah made her demand (Gen 21:10), Abraham got upset (Gen 21:11), God reassuringly told him to do what Sarah had asked (Gen 21:12–13), and Abraham obeyed (Gen 21:14).

However, this small test of Abraham's attachment to Ishmael foreshadows the even greater test to come. As one scholar notes, "We readers … should not underestimate the difficulty Abraham probably had in, as it were, 'sacrificing' Ishmael, his firstborn, the first bearer of his great hope for posterity."[4] Ishmael had been part of Abraham's life for at least 13 years. Abraham's reluctance to satisfy Sarah's demand is understandable, but he obeyed and sent Hagar and Ishmael away after receiving God's reassurance: Isaac was the child of promise and Ishmael would be safe, though separated from him.

The next and ultimate test of Abraham's devotion and love for his sons comes several years later (as indicated by the ambiguous transition "and it happened that after these things" in Gen 22:1). However the story explicitly identifies the entire scene that follows as a test, stating, "God tested Abraham" (Gen 22:1). This small piece of information is intended to alleviate the reader's horror at what is to come. Abraham, however, did not know that it was only a test.

**Quick Bit:** The Hebrew word for "test," *nissah*, often refers to putting something (or someone) under scrutiny, usually to determine its value or usefulness. For example, David decided not to use Saul's armor because he hadn't tested it (1 Sam 17:39). God often tests our faith for a positive purpose (Exod 20:20; Deut 8:16); he tested the Israelites to determine whether they fully trusted in God alone (Deut 13:3). The righteous invite such testing (Psa 26:2), while the wicked are punished for testing God (Num 14:22). "God tests to identify his people, to discern who is serious about faith and to know in whose lives he will be fully God."[5]

God commanded Abraham to take Isaac to Moriah and sacrifice him— his beloved son—as a burnt offering (Gen 21:2). If Abraham had ever felt at liberty to question God (Gen 18:22–33), surely it would have been on this occasion. But instead, Abraham obeyed without question. The narrative methodically describes Abraham's actions: He got up early, saddled the donkey, cut wood for the sacrifice, took Isaac and two servants, and headed for Moriah—all without speaking a word. Shouldn't he have told Sarah where they were going and that it might be the last time she saw her son? Couldn't he have asked God for an explanation? God's command to sacrifice Isaac directly contradicted the promise that "through Isaac your offspring will be named" (Gen 21:12). Did this contradiction provide enough of a clue for Abraham to recognize that God was only testing him? If this were the case, however, then it wouldn't have qualified as a test. Abraham's actions could not have demonstrated extreme faith unless he felt he was truly taking a risk by obeying God.

The nature of God's command should trouble us; the entire ethic of the Bible as a whole opposes human sacrifice (see Lev 18:21; 2 Kgs 3:27). How, then, do we make sense of this unexpected turn of events? Abraham's life consistently alternated between affirming and jeopardizing God's promise to him. With Isaac, the promise had seemingly been fulfilled, which prompts us to question: Where would Abraham place his trust now? In the fulfillment of the promise in the birth of Isaac? Or in God's power to fulfill the promise in the future, no matter what? As Abraham's final test of faith, the sacrifice of Isaac required that he once again place his hope in God's hands. Just like before, the focus of the event is the endangered promise, which now happens to be embodied in a living, breathing person: Isaac.

The narrative continues in its methodical descriptions of Abraham's every move. After three days of traveling, he "lifted up his eyes and saw" the place where he would sacrifice Isaac (Gen 22:4). He then took Isaac ahead, but only after telling his servants, "You stay here with the donkey, and I and the boy will go up there. We will worship, then we will return to you" (Gen 22:5). Did Abraham fully expect that God would resurrect Isaac and that they would return together? Or was he merely hiding the truth of what he was about to do?

As Abraham and Isaac continued on, Isaac carried the wood for the sacrifice, indicating that he had grown significantly since his last appearance in the story (see Gen 21:8). He also appeared to be familiar with the process of sacrifice since he pointed out that they didn't have a lamb for the offering (Gen 22:7). Abraham's response provides the key to understanding this entire event: "God will provide the lamb for a burnt offering" (Gen 22:8). The test hinged on the tension between God's past provision and his promise to provide in the future.

As the story reaches its climax, the tension plays out in another detailed account of Abraham's actions. He built an altar, arranged the wood, bound Isaac, placed him on the altar, stretched out his hand, and brandished his knife for the killing blow (Gen 22:9–10). Abraham and Isaac exchanged no words. Isaac was a passive participant, neither explicitly agreeing to the plan nor fighting for his fate.

> Few narratives in Genesis can equal this story in dramatic tension. The writer seems deliberately to prolong the tension of both Abraham and the reader in his depiction of the last moments before God interrupted the action and called the test to a halt.[6]

At Genesis 22:10, Abraham had passed the test. An angel appeared, bearing a message from God that halted the sacrifice and acknowledged the depth of Abraham's faith. Abraham had demonstrated his trust in God's power to provide for him and ensure the success of the promise. The expected outcome of death became the unexpected miracle of life.

The success of this final test was recognized by another pronouncement of God's covenant promises for Abraham. God reaffirmed his promise to bless Abraham with descendants as numerous as the stars in the sky, and to bless the entire world through Abraham's offspring. Just as it began, the story of Abraham ends with this promise of worldwide blessing (Gen 12:3; 22:18).

God's initial promise to Abraham appeared unconditional. Nothing was required of Abraham for him to receive this blessing. However, over the course of multiple reiterations of the promise, God established that Abraham's faithful obedience was a condition of his continued blessing. The test to sacrifice Isaac was the final proof of Abraham's commitment to cling to God's voice and follow his promise, no matter where it led or what it required (Gen 22:18).

## THROUGHOUT THE BIBLE

Abraham's willingness to sacrifice Isaac represents the highest expression of his faith in Genesis. The authors of the NT similarly recognized this event as a preeminent example of faithfully responding to God. The author of Hebrews emphasizes how Abraham serves as an example for believers, writing, "the one who received the promises was ready to offer his one and only son" (Heb 11:17). The very tension we identified earlier is present here: While God's command to sacrifice Isaac seemed to jeopardize God's promise to him, Abraham "was ready." His example encourages us to "run with patient endurance the race that has been set before us" (Heb 12:1).

While the author of Hebrews uses the story to point to Abraham's faith, James refers to this event with a slightly different focus. In writing "Was not Abraham our father justified by works when he offered up his son Isaac on the altar?" (Jas 2:21), we are led to ask whether James is promoting a salvation by works. At first glance, it may appear so. However, James is actually arguing that true faith makes itself evident through works. He continues by stating that Abraham's faith was *perfected* by his willingness to sacrifice Isaac (Jas 2:22). Abraham's actions served as the evidence, not the means, of his salvation.

**Quick Bit:** Understanding Isaac as a foreshadowing of Christ represents a form of biblical interpretation called "typology." Typology considers select characters and events of the OT to prefigure and find their ultimate fulfillment in Christ. A trademark of biblical interpretation during the periods of the early church and the Middle Ages, typology regarded people like Moses and Jonah (along with Isaac) as prefigures of Christ. Theologically, typology was fueled by the idea that all of history points to and finds its full significance in Christ.

The authors of the NT also believed Abraham's willingness to sacrifice Isaac fore-shadowed the sacrifice of Jesus on the cross. Hebrews describes Isaac as Abraham's "one and only son" (Heb 11:17). The Greek term here, *monogenēs*, is used most often in the NT to describe Jesus, God's only begotten Son (see John 1:14; 3:16). Paul also describes God's sending of Christ to redeem humanity as "he did not spare his own Son" (Rom 8:32), phrasing that echoes God's words to Abraham in Genesis 22:16.

While the sacrifice of Isaac came to be understood as foreshadowing Christ's sacrifice, there was one major difference: Isaac was spared, whereas Christ was sacrificed. Abraham was willing to sacrifice his only son, but God intervened and provided a substitute for Isaac in the form of the ram (Gen 22:13). God loves us enough that he did not spare his only Son; instead, Christ took our place as *our* substitute. And through the sacrifice of Christ, we have become heirs of the promise God first gave to Abraham and fulfilled through the redemption of Christ (Rom 8:17).

## BEYOND THE BIBLE

When we encounter testing, we often want an explanation. We retrace our steps to figure out what led to our difficult situation. The author of *Targum Pseudo Jonathan*—an Aramaic translation of the Hebrew Pentateuch—did the same thing. He provided his version of the backstory to explain God's test in Genesis 22.

**Quick Bit:** The name "Targum" comes from the Aramaic word *trgm*, meaning "to explain or translate." The Targums are a series of Aramaic translations of the Hebrew Bible (the OT). *Targum Pseudo Jonathan*, which is named for its alleged author, Jonathan ben Uzziel, contains explanatory expansions to the Pentateuch. Although it includes material from the last few centuries BC and early centuries

AD, it wasn't brought together as a whole until the seventh or eighth century AD.[7]

The author attributed the events of Genesis 22 to a quarrel between Abraham's sons, Ishmael and Isaac. As the two men argued about their status as heirs, Ishmael asserted his supremacy on the basis of his righteousness: He did not refuse God's painful command to be circumcised at the age of 13 (see Gen 17:25). Isaac was only eight days old when he was circumcised, and he did not have a choice in the matter (see Gen 21:4); Ishmael claimed that had Isaac been older, he may have refused to comply with God's command (see Gen 17:9–14). Isaac resented this accusation and replied, "Behold, today I'm 37 years old. If the Holy One—blessed is he—should ask, I would not withhold any of my members."[8] Upon hearing this, God decided to test both Abraham *and* Isaac. The results would determine the rightful heir.

According to this account, neither Abraham nor Isaac knew the reason for God's test, but both were determined to prove their devotion to him through extreme faith. When Abraham grabbed the knife to sacrifice his son, Issac said, "Bind me well so that I will not kick convulsively from pain of death and be cast into the pit of destruction, and make your sacrifice unfit."[9] These dual acts of righteous devotion—Abraham's willingness to kill his promised son and Isaac's obedience to the point of death—amazed the angels so much that they watched from heaven and marveled.

But like the biblical story, neither man knew the reason for their test. The point in both cases—and with any retelling of the story—is this: Abraham responded to God's instructions with extreme faith; he knew *what* God asked, but not *why*. And God honored his response of faith, which now serves as an example for us. With or without the explanatory expansions of *Targum Pseudo Jonathan*, experiences like Abraham's provide us with the courage we need to respond in extreme faith even in the most difficult circumstances.

## APPLICATION

Abraham's life is bracketed by examples of extreme faith. In Genesis 12:1, God told him to go to a foreign land, and in Genesis 12:4, he obeyed without question. He left all he knew for the sake of obtaining God's promise. In Genesis 22, after he finally received the promised son, Abraham was commanded to give Isaac up as a burnt offering. Despite the apparent absurdity of the request, Abraham complied without ever questioning God. He was confident that both he and Isaac would return—whether by resurrection or some other form of deliverance (see Heb 11:19).

Despite his failures along the way, Abraham is remembered for these two successes—particularly his unflinching faith in Genesis 22. After walking with God for 25 years, Abraham knew God could be trusted. Sacrificing Isaac wasn't the first seemingly "crazy" thing God asked him to do. God had commanded Abraham to leave the comforts of home and spend his life sojourning in tents; he had instructed him to travel with his family among potentially hostile enemies; he had ordered him to circumcise himself as a sign of his covenant of "blessing"; he had directed him to cast out his true firstborn son, Ishmael; and he had told him to conceive a child at the age of 100. Yet Abraham trusted God's purposes through all these things and, in Genesis 22, he complied without hesitation with God's most shocking demand yet.

Not only was God's reputation for keeping his covenant at stake—he would have to undergo something similar in the future. Approximately 2,000 years later, in a situation that mirrored Abraham's, God offered his own Son as a sacrifice for the sins of humanity. This connection is what makes Genesis 22 so real for us. Abraham could have looked for an easy way out just as he did earlier in his life, but he didn't. He had come to know God's power and trusted him to fulfill his promises.

God commands us to trust in the sacrifice of his Son, and this can sometimes be difficult. There are certainly easier ways to get through life— ways that will allow for the kind of compromise and dishonesty that we observed earlier in Abraham's story. But none of these will get us where God wants us to be: with him for eternity. Walter Brueggemann, a theologian and Bible commentator, summed up the situation well:

> The testing times for Israel and for all of us who are heirs of Abraham are those times when it is seductively attractive to find an easier, less demanding alternative to God. The testings which come in history (and which are from God) drive us to find out whether

we mean what we say about our faith being grounded solely in the gospel.[1]

Following God is difficult, but Abraham knew he could trust God no matter what kind of test emerged. The same is true for us today. When our commitment is tested, we can look to examples like Abraham for the courage to persevere (see Rom 15:4; 1 Cor 10:11; Heb 12:1–3). The same God who provided for Abraham in his most desperate hour (see Gen 22:13) also makes deliverance possible for us (see John 3:16–17). As true children of Abraham—followers of God characterized by faith—we can demonstrate our devotion by an extreme faith in God's promises and sacrifice.

## DISCUSSION

### A Closer Look

1. Have you ever experienced a time when you were more focused on what God had provided for you in the past than on what he might have planned for you in the future?

_____

_____

_____

2. Reflect on a time when you felt your faith was being tested. What made it difficult or easy for you to believe?

_____

_____

_____

### Throughout the Bible

1. Read James 2:14-26 and Romans 4:1-25. How do you understand the interplay of faith and works as explained by James and Paul? What relevance does this have in your life?

_____

_____

_____

2. In what ways does Abraham's willingness to sacrifice Isaac remind you of Christ's sacrifice? In what ways are these sacrifices different?

_____

_____

_____

**Beyond the Bible**

1. Can you think of a time when God called on you to exhibit extreme faith? How did you do it, and what was the result?

_____

_____

_____

2. Think of an instance where you witnessed God's deliverance in the midst of a struggle or trial. How did he deliver, and what did you learn about his character?

_____

_____

_____

**Application**

1. How does the example of Abraham's faith encourage you in your walk with God? How does God's faithfulness to his promise strengthen your faith?

_____

_____

_____

2. Read Hebrews 12:1–3. How does the hostility Jesus endured affect your faith? How will remembering Christ's sacrifice help you in times of testing?

_____

_____

_____

# CONCLUSION

It's no accident that we remember Abraham as a champion of faith—he rightfully holds a prominent place among those we recognize as exemplary models of faithful living (Heb 11). Yet he, more than most biblical characters, also shows that following God's promise—accepting God's word and trusting him in all circumstances—involves real human struggle. Looking closely at Abraham's life reveals that he experienced the same difficulties with sin that we do as we strive to follow God. Time and again, he encountered the same tension we do between being "set free from sin" (Rom 6:18) and being "captive to the law of sin" (Rom 7:23). His journey of faith powerfully demonstrates that faithful living does not require perfect behavior.

Abraham even had a distinct advantage—he directly communicated with God. Yet he still stumbled. He still doubted that God would follow through on his promises. He often tried to find his own solutions when God wouldn't give him the details. Abraham serves as a profound model of faith for us *not* because he was perfect, but because he was persistent. Despite his struggles and continual need for reassurance, he kept returning to the path of faith. Eventually, he understood that God would be faithful to his promises, regardless of his own understanding. But Abraham only understood this after numerous, repeated blunders, such as putting his wife in danger twice, questioning God's ability to do the impossible, and doubting God's plans for his sons.

Abraham's story also helps us look beyond our individual attempts to live in faithful response to God's call; it points us toward God's redemption of the world. The initiation of God's plan of salvation comes into sharper focus throughout Genesis 12–25. Abraham's call in Genesis 12:1–3 contains the essential foreshadowing of the gospel: "And all families of the earth will be blessed in you" (Gen 12:3b). From that point on, God's plan to save all people was intimately connected with his plan for Israel. When Abraham—from his early vantage point—struggled to comprehend the intricate workings of fulfillment and blessing, God provided him with reassurance: He gave Abraham details of his future plans for his descendants (Gen 15:13) and voiced his intention to give Abraham land and a son (Gen 17:8, 21).

Perhaps Abraham's greatest struggle was accepting God's timing. He waited 25 years to see the initial fulfillment of God's promise of a son, which shows us that God's timing rarely aligns with our expectations or wants. In the same way, thousands of years passed before God fulfilled his promise of future victory over sin by sending his son (see Gen 3:15; John 3:16; Gal 4:4). In that fulfillment of Christ, we learn that God asked nothing less of Abraham than what he was himself willing to give. Just as God provided the sacrifice for Abraham (Gen 22:8), so God himself provided the sacrifice that would result in his promised blessing of salvation. Abraham's experiences of God's grace enabled Jesus to declare that the very essence of the gospel was revealed to Abraham (John 8:56).

The presence of God's grace in Abraham's life has made his story compelling throughout history, and it continues to make him compelling for us today. Our journey of following God's promises mirrors Abraham's; we navigate the same twists and turns, ups and downs, false starts, and U-turns. Yet we can find encouragement in knowing that living by faith doesn't require perfection—just persistence.

# NOTES

## Chapter 1

1. Some English Bibles translate Genesis 12:1 to say that God "*had said to Abram*" (Gen 12:1 KJV), using the past perfect tense to reflect their understanding that the call occurred back in Ur.
2. Samuel Rapaport, *Tales and Maxims from the Midrash* (New York: E. P. Dutton, 1907), 68.
3. Jacob Neusner, *The Babylonian Talmud: A Translation and Commentary* (Peabody, MA: Hendrickson, 2011), 15:271.
4. Louis Ginzberg et al., *Legends of the Jews*, 2nd ed. (Philadelphia: Jewish Publication Society, 2003), 170.
5. Ibid., 173.
6. Rapaport, *Tales and Maxims*, 68.

## Chapter 2

1. Adapted from James Pritchard, ed., "The Report of a Frontier Official," in *Ancient Near Eastern Texts Relating to the Old Testament* (Princeton: Princeton University Press, 1958), 259.
2. Miriam Lichtheim, Ancient Egyptian Literature Vol. 1: The Old and Middle Kingdoms (Berkeley: University of California Press, 1973), 154-55.
3. Excerpts of the *Genesis Apocryphon* from Florentino Garcia Martinez, ed., *About the Dead Sea Scrolls Study Edition (Translations)*, Vol. 1 (New York: Brill, 1997-1998), 40-44.

## Chapter 3

1. For a more detailed discussion of the locations for Sodom and Gomorrah, see Chapter 6 "Setting the Stage."
2. Victor P. Hamilton, *The Book of Genesis: Chapters 1-17* (Grand Rapids: Eerdmans, 1990), 409.
3. E. A. Speiser, *Genesis* (New Haven: Yale University Press, 2008), 104.
4. Gordon J. Wenham, *Word Biblical Commentary Vol. 1: Genesis 1-15* (Dallas: Word, Inc., 2002), 317.
5. Adapted from Geza Vermes, "The Heavenly Prince Melchizedek (11QMelch)," Col. ii, lines 24-25, in *The Dead Sea Scrolls in English*, rev. and extended 4th ed. (Sheffield: Sheffield Academic Press, 1995), 362.
6. Ibid., Col. ii, lines 9-10. 361.
7. Ibid., Col. ii, line 6. 361.

## Chapter 4

1. James Pritchard, ed., *Ancient Near Eastern Texts Relating to the Old Testament* (ANET) (Princeton: Princeton University Press, 1958), 543.
2. Ibid., 220.
3. Ibid., Lipit-Ishtar Lawcode, 160.
4. Ibid., Code of Hammurabi, 172.
5. Abram was 75 years old when he left Haran (Gen 12:4) and 86 years old when Hagar gave birth to Ishmael (Gen 16:16).
6. John H. Sailhamer, "Genesis," in *The Expositor's Bible Commentary, Vol. 2: Genesis, Exodus, Leviticus, Numbers*, ed. Frank E. Gaebelein (Grand Rapids: Zondervan, 1990), 129.
7. Rom 4:3, 5 (2x), 9, 11, 12, 13, 16, 17, 18, 19, 20. See Nancy Calvert-Koyzis, *Paul, Monotheism and the People of God: The Significance of Abraham Traditions for Early Judaism and Christianity* (London: T&T Clark International, 2004), 135.
8. Calvert-Koyzis, 93. Jewish tradition claims that "Abraham kept the entire Torah even before it was revealed" (*m. Qidd.* 4.14).
9. Mark Sheridan, "Homilies on Genesis," in *Genesis 12–50* (Downers Grove, IL: InterVarsity Press, 2002), 30.
10. Ibid., 31.
11. Ibid.

## Chapter 5

1. In addition to omnipotence, God is also traditionally attributed with complete goodness (omnibenevolence), knowledge of all things (omniscience), and being present everywhere (omnipresence).
2. *b. Shabbat* 127A, quoted from Jacob Neusner, *The Babylonian Talmud: A Translation and Commentary* (Peabody, MA: Hendrickson, 2011), 586.
3. *Antiquities* 1.198, quoted from Flavius Josephus, et al., *Flavius Josephus: Translation and Commentary, Vol. 3: Judean Antiquities Books 1–4* (Boston: Brill, 2000), 75.
4. F. L. Cross and Elizabeth A. Livingstone, *The Oxford Dictionary of the Christian Church*, 3rd ed. rev. (Oxford: Oxford University Press, 2005), 1288.
5. Philo of Alexandria and Charles Duke Yonge, "On Abraham 142–43," in *The Works of Philo: Complete and Unabridged* (Peabody, MA: Hendrickson, 1995) 423.

## Chapter 6

1. Steven Collins, "Sodom and the Cities of the Plain," in *Lexham Bible Dictionary*, John D. Barry et al., eds., (Bellingham, WA: Logos Bible Software, 2012).
2. Steven Collins and Hussein Aljarrah, "The Tell el-Hammam Excavation Project: End of Season Activity Report—Season Six: 2011 Excavation, Exploration, and Survey" (filed with the Jordan Department of Antiquities, 26 January 2011), 11.
3. David literally says, "Far be it from me from the Lord." Most English translations render this phrase as "The LORD forbid" (ESV; NIV).
4. Nahum M. Sarna, "The Character of Abraham; The Nature of God (vv. 1–33)" and "The Destruction of Sodom and Gomorrah (vv. 1–35)" in *Genesis: The JPS Torah Commentary* (Philadelphia: Jewish Publication Society, 1989), 128–139.
5. Allen Ross and John Oswalt Ross, *Cornerstone Biblical Commentary, Vol. 1: Genesis, Exodus* (Carol Stream, IL: Tyndale House, 2008), 127.
6. Note that Job repented in "dust and ashes" (Job 42:6). This is the same phrase Abraham used to describe himself as he spoke to God (Gen 18:27).
7. See the discussion on Genesis 18:22–33 in Sarna, *Genesis: The JPS Torah Commentary*, 132–33.

8. James Pritchard, ed., "I Will Praise the Lord of Wisdom (2.32–41)," in *Ancient Near Eastern Texts Relating to the Old Testament (ANET)*, (Princeton, NJ: Princeton University Press, 1958), 597.

## Chapter 7

1. Nahum M. Sarna, *Genesis: The JPS Torah Commentary* (Philadelphia, PA: Jewish Publication Society, 1989), 141.
2. Ibid., 142.
3. William David Reyburn and Euan McG. Fry, *A Handbook on Genesis*, UBS Handbook Series (New York: United Bible Societies, 1998), 453.
4. Jacob Neusner, *The Babylonian Talmud: A Translation and Commentary* (Peabody, MA: Hendrickson, 2011). Cited by Nahum M. Sarna, *Genesis: The JPS Torah Commentary* (Philadelphia: Jewish Publication Society, 1989), 141.

## Chapter 8

1. A. F. Rainey, "Sacrifice," in *The Zondervan Encyclopedia of the Bible, Vol. 5, Q–Z*, eds. Moisés Silva and Merrill Chapin Tenney (Grand Rapids: Zondervan, 2009), 235.
2. These examples all reflect sacrificial practices prior to the outlining of formal rules for sacrifice in the Mosaic law.
3. The author of Hebrews mentions that Abraham believed God could raise Isaac from the dead (Heb 11:19).
4. Leon R. Kass, *The Beginning of Wisdom: Reading Genesis* (New York: Free Press, 2003), 332.
5. Walter Brueggemann, *Genesis: Interpretation: A Bible Commentary for Teaching and Preaching* (Atlanta: John Knox Press, 1982), 193.
6. John H. Sailhamer, "Genesis," in *The Expositor's Bible Commentary, Vol. 2: Genesis, Exodus, Leviticus, Numbers*, ed. Frank E. Gaebelein (Grand Rapids: Zondervan, 1990), 169.
7. Information in this paragraph from S. D. Fraade, "Targum, Targumim," in *The Eerdmans Dictionary of Early Judaism*, eds. J. J. Collins and D. C. Harlow (Grand Rapids; Eerdmans, 2010), 1278–81; and P. S. Alexander, "Targum, Targumim," in *The Anchor Yale Bible Dictionary, Vol. 6*, ed. D. N. Freedman (New York: Doubleday, 1992), 320–31.
8. Author's translation from Comprehensive Aramaic Lexicon. *Targum Pseudo-Jonathan to the Pentateuch*. Hebrew Union College, 2005.
9. Author's translation from Ibid.
10. Brueggemann, 190.

# SOURCES

Alexander, T. Desmond, and David W. Baker. *Dictionary of the Old Testament: Pentateuch.* Downers Grove, IL: InterVarsity Press, 2003.

Barry, John D., and Lazarus Wentz. *Lexham Bible Dictionary.* Bellingham, WA: Logos Bible Software, 2012.

Bromiley, Geoffrey W., ed. *The International Standard Bible Encyclopedia, Revised.* Grand Rapids: Eerdmans, 1988.

Brueggemann, Walter. *Genesis: Interpretation: A Bible Commentary for Teaching and Preaching.* Atlanta: John Knox Press, 1982.

Calvert-Koyzis, Nancy. *Paul, Monotheism and the People of God: The Significance of Abraham Traditions for Early Judaism and Christianity.* London: T&T Clark International, 2004.

Collins, John J. and Daniel C. Harlow. *The Eerdmans Dictionary of Early Judaism.* Grand Rapids: Eerdmans, 2010.

Collins, Steven, and Hussein Aljarrah. "The Tall el-Hammam Excavation Project: End of Season Activity Report—Season Six: 2011 Excavation, Exploration, and Survey." Filed with the Jordan Department of Antiquities, 26 January 2011.

Comprehensive Aramaic Lexicon. *Targum Pseudo-Jonathan to the Pentateuch.* Hebrew Union College, 2005.

Cross, F. L., and Elizabeth A. Livingstone. *The Oxford Dictionary of the Christian Church.* 3rd ed. rev. Oxford: Oxford University Press, 2005.

De Haan, M. R. *Adventures in Faith: Studies in the Life of Abraham.* Grand Rapids: Kregel Publications, 1996.

Freedman, David Noel, and Gary A. Herion, David F. Graf, et al., eds. *The Anchor Yale Bible Dictionary.* New York: Doubleday, 1992.

Freedman, David Noel, Allen C. Myers, and Astrid B. Beck. *The Eerdmans Dictionary of the Bible.* Grand Rapids: Eerdmans, 2000.

García Martínez, Florentino, and Eibert J. C. Tigchelaar. *The Dead Sea Scrolls Study Edition*. 2 vols. Leiden: Brill, 1997–1998.

Ginzberg, Louis, Henrietta Szold, and Paul Radin. *Legends of the Jews*. 2nd ed. Philadelphia: Jewish Publication Society, 2003.

Gower, Ralph. *The New Manners & Customs of Bible Times*. Chicago: Moody Press, 2005.

Hamilton, Victor P. "The Book of Genesis, Chapters 1–17." *The New International Commentary on the Old Testament*. Grand Rapids: Eerdmans, 1990.

———. "The Book of Genesis, Chapters 18–50." *The New International Commentary on the Old Testament*. Grand Rapids: Eerdmans, 1995.

Janzen, J. Gerald. *Abraham and All the Families of the Earth: A Commentary on the Book of Genesis 12–50*. Grand Rapids: Eerdmans, 1993.

Josephus, Flavius, Steve Mason, and Louis H. Feldman. *Flavius Josephus: Translation and Commentary, Vol. 3: Judean Antiquities Books 1–4*. Leiden: Brill, 2000.

Kass, Leon R. *The Beginning of Wisdom: Reading Genesis*. New York: Free Press, 2003.

Lichtheim, Miriam. *Ancient Egyptian Literature: Vol. I: The Old and Middle Kingdoms*. Berkeley: University of California Press, 1973.

Mathews, K. A. "Genesis 11:27–50:26." *The New American Commentary*, Vol. 1B. Nashville: Broadman & Holman Publishers, 2005.

Neusner, Jacob. *The Babylonian Talmud: A Translation and Commentary*. Peabody, MA: Hendrickson, 2011.

———. *Introduction to Rabbinic Literature*. New Haven: Yale University Press, 1994.

Philo of Alexandria, and Charles Duke Yonge. *The Works of Philo: Complete and Unabridged*. Peabody, MA: Hendrickson, 1995.

Pritchard, James Bennett, ed. *The Ancient Near East: An Anthology of Texts and Pictures*. Princeton: Princeton University Press, 1958.

Rapaport, Samuel. *Tales and Maxims from the Midrash*. New York: E. P. Dutton, 1907.

Reyburn, William David, and Euan McG. Fry. *A Handbook on Genesis*. UBS Handbook Series. New York: United Bible Societies, 1998.

Ross, Allen, and John N. Oswalt. *Cornerstone Biblical Commentary, Vol. 1: Genesis, Exodus*. Carol Stream, IL: Tyndale House Publishers, 2008.

Ross, Allen P. *Creation and Blessing: A Guide to the Study and Exposition of Genesis*. Grand Rapids: Baker Books, 1998.

Sailhamer, John H. "Genesis." In *The Expositor's Bible Commentary, Vol. 2: Genesis, Exodus, Leviticus, Numbers.* Edited by Frank E. Gaebelein. Grand Rapids: Zondervan, 1990.

Sarna, Nahum M. "Genesis." *The JPS Torah Commentary.* Philadelphia: Jewish Publication Society, 1989.

Sheridan, Mark. "Genesis 12–50." *Ancient Christian Commentary on Scripture OT 2.* Downers Grove, IL: InterVarsity Press, 2002.

Silva, Moisés, and Merrill Chapin Tenney. *The Zondervan Encyclopedia of the Bible.* 5 vols. Rev., Full-Color Edition. Grand Rapids: Zondervan, 2009.

Speiser, E. A. "Genesis: Introduction, Translation, and Notes." *Anchor Yale Bible Commentary,* Vol. 1. New Haven: Yale University Press, 2008.

Vermes, Geza. *The Dead Sea Scrolls in English.* Rev. and extended 4th ed. Sheffield: Sheffield Academic Press, 1995.

Walton, John H. *Zondervan Illustrated Bible Backgrounds Commentary (Old Testament) Volume 1: Genesis, Exodus, Leviticus, Numbers, Deuteronomy.* Grand Rapids: Zondervan, 2009.

Wenham, Gordon J. "Genesis 1–15." *Word Biblical Commentary,* Vol. 1. Dallas: Word, 1998.

———. "Genesis 16–50." *Word Biblical Commentary,* Vol. 2. Dallas: Word, 1998.

# ABOUT THE EDITOR AND COAUTHOR

**Michael R. Grigoni** has served as managing editor of Bible Reference at Lexham Press. He is the editor of *Mary: Devoted to God's Plan* and two other Studies in Faithful Living volumes. He holds a Master of Theological Studies from Harvard Divinity School. Previously, Michael has served as a trained hospital chaplain, assisted in pastoring, and led worship for large congregations.

# ABOUT THE AUTHORS

**Miles Custis** is the author of *The End of the Matter: Understanding the Epilogue of Ecclesiastes*, a Faithlife Study Bible contributing editor, the coauthor of Lexham Bible Guides: Genesis Collection, and the coauthor of *Jacob: Discerning God's Presence* and three other Studies in Faithful Living volumes. He holds a Master of Arts in biblical studies from Trinity Western University.

**Douglas Mangum** is the editor of the Lexham Bible Guides series and the Lexham Methods Series. He is the coauthor of Lexham Bible Guides: Genesis Collection, *Joseph: Understanding God's Purpose* and three other Studies in Faithful Living volumes. He is a Lexham English Bible editor, a Faithlife Study Bible contributing editor, a regular *Bible Study Magazine* contributor, and a frequently consulted specialist for the *Lexham Bible Dictionary*. In addition, he is a PhD candidate in Near Eastern studies at the University of Free State; he holds a Master of Arts in Hebrew and Semitic studies from the University of Wisconsin–Madison.

**Matthew M. Whitehead** is the coauthor of *Lexham Bible Guide: Ephesians* and three Studies in Faithful Living volumes. He has also served as a Faithlife Study Bible contributing editor. He assisted with the digitization process for the Discoveries in the Judaean Desert series and worked on the Oxford Hebrew Bible project. Matthew holds an MDiv from Northwest Baptist Seminary and is pursuing an MA in biblical studies at Trinity Western University.

# ABRAHAM
## FOLLOWING GOD'S PROMISE

Keep studying Abraham with your entire church: pick up the complete digital curriculum

### Personal workbook

Biblical, cultural, and historical background, plus applications and reflection questions

### Leader's guide

The key to the complete curriculum, with sermon outlines and downloads for media and handouts

### Presentation slides

Both sermon and small group versions available in PowerPoint and Keynote, standard and high definition

### Sermon outlines

Weekly lesson outlines and discussion questions, with space for notes and reflections

### Group handouts

Key passages, learning objectives, and prompts for slides and videos, available in Word and PDF

### Videos

Introductory videos for each week's session—plus a bumper video to promote the series

*Abraham: Following God's Promise Church Curriculum* helps your entire church dig deeper into the life of Abraham. Plus, our digital resources sync across platforms, so you can take your study with you anytime, anywhere.

## Equip your church today!

LexhamPress.com/SFL-Abraham  ◦  1-800-875-6467 (US)  ◦  +1 360-527-1700 (Int'l)

**LEXHAM PRESS**

LOGOS
Bible Software